SELF-MASTERY
—&—
MENTAL HEALTH
2-Books-in-1

A Guide to Self-Mastery + Mental Health   Mental Peace

How to Relieve Stress and Anxiety, and Change Your Life Through
The Law of Attraction, Meditation, Master Key System,
Thought Control and Visualization

Tammy Gallagher, FNLP

Contents

Mental Health – Mental Peace

A Guide to Self-Mastery

MENTAL
HEALTH
MENTAL PEACE

A Practical Guide To Reducing
Stress, Relieving Anxiety,
Decluttering the Mind, and
Being Happy

Tammy Gallagher, FNLP

$\mathcal{A}$ $\mathcal{W}$ord from the $\mathcal{A}$uthor

I came across this quote by Marisa Peer: "*The most important words you will ever hear are the words you say to yourself. So, make them positive. Make them kind.*" And it's changed my view on many things in life, and mostly, it changed my perspective on how I think.

Indeed, this behavioral therapist and the author must have made an interesting observation of her personal life. Is it possible that she thought: 'My mind is a very negative place. I am always thinking about the worst and undesirable things.' But then, I'm sure she must have often experienced that deep sense of peace and happiness. And that's when she realized: 'What a difference it makes to say positive things to your mind!'

I like that this quote is not just practical but insightful. How often have we experienced that feeling of peace and contentment, only to think: *'Why doesn't it happen more often? How can I make it happen more often? Is it possible to have this feeling all the time?'* The subconscious mind has the power to make it happen more often. But how can we get the subconscious mind on our side? Can we program it to think positively? It turns out that, yes, we can.

Mental health isn't just about avoiding burnout at the workplace, going to school without anxiety, becoming stress-free, decluttering the mind, or unblocking the mental drain of negativity. It's about much more such as self-improvement, ambitions and goals, relationships, gratitude, and deep inner understanding and acceptance.

Mental health is a skill, like sports, playing an instrument, or dancing. And, like them, it requires practice and training. But fortunately for us all, we don't need to enroll in an evening class on Yoga or a session at the gym. We can practice Mental Health in the comfort of our homes, at work, or at school. And we can use this skill to change our lives and surroundings as we please.

I'm writing this book not just for people who suffer from psychological challenges like stress, anxiety, or depression. I'm writing this book for people who take life seriously – the ones who want to live on purpose, by their sense of values and goals in life. And to make that happen, they need a tool to help them live a happy and healthy life.

We need a way to tame that negative voice that whispers in our ears, telling us that we can't do it and we shouldn't even try to. Or that voice that spins everything negatively. We need a way to keep the cheerful voice that says: *'You can do it; you must do it.'* And most importantly, we need a way to keep it going! We need a way to set a mental reminder: *'Don't forget that you're a person with a right to live life to the fullest. You deserve it, and you can do it. And while you're at it, you can be the happiest you have ever been.'*

That's what this book is all about. It's a guide to self-development, inner peace, and happiness. It's meant to help people live the life they want. The kind of life they love and can be proud of! And it won't come around if we don't do something about it – if we don't take control of that one part of ourselves that can make it happen. That part of ourselves is our mind, and it can be changed without surgery or medication.

And so, welcome to the journey into self-mastery! Let's start by learning how to get in touch with our subconscious mind and programming it to direct us on the path toward happiness, glory, and fulfillment.

This book is meant for everyone who wants to live a fuller life than they are. Are you ready to get started?

I wish you all the best and hope you pick up at least a few tidbits that help you achieve *Mental Peace.*

Cheers,

About the Author

Life has a way of leading us to our fate, and Tammy Gallagher's life was no exception. She became overweight in her twenties, developed high blood pressure and high cholesterol, and developed Crohn's disease in her late forties. She spent most of her adult life in the residential development industry but found herself leaving the industry in 2018 as she realized she was trading her health for money. She was operating on autopilot and wasn't happy, so she sought to change.

Tammy learned that 'giving up' is never an option, and she finally returned to college in her fifties to get the degree she wanted. Tammy is a functional nutrition and lifestyle practitioner and author; best yet, she received her health and life back. She now shares the wisdom gained from her experience with others as a means of encouragement and support.

In 2018 Tammy decided that she wanted to give back more to the world than she had been able to do by continuing her journey toward mastering a healthy body and mind. She opened Ballantyne Weight Loss Center to help others achieve health as well.

As a businesswoman, Tammy understands that changing one's life requires vision, determination, and perseverance. This book aims to provide people with inspiration and advice on how to live a healthier lifestyle by improving their mental health to reach their full potential: physically, mentally, emotionally, and spiritually.

www.tamgall.com

Forward

This book is for those looking to find a way to become happier and more fulfilled in life. It is designed to open the mind, influence how you think, and ultimately improve your quality of life.

The number of examples throughout separates this book from many other self-help books on the market. These show that you don't have to be perfect or utterly healthy before embarking on such a journey. The goal is simple – if you make one change or two simple ones, your life can improve significantly for the better immediately.

If you're mildly stressed or have anxiety about an upcoming event, I can help. Still, there will be material in this book for others who are further down the road with stress, anxiety, depression, or other mental disorders; I can help them too. And finally, a few will want advice on taking your life and happiness to the next level. I haven't forgotten you. There is a wide variety of areas of improvement regarding mental health. My objective is to give you a resource, regardless of where you are in your journey, that can travel with you as you continue to grow or stumble and that you can rely upon to support mental health.

However, none of what I offer will help you if you have already decided it won't. If you're stressed, have anxiety, or can't stop the thoughts from going over and over in your mind, you must understand that your current thoughts have contributed to where you are today. Approach this material with an open mind because it is a change in your mind that will create improved results.

Is This Book for You?

1.   Are you looking for a happier, healthier life?

Holistic wellness is about achieving balance for a happier, healthier life. It isn't about obsessing over one area of your life but balancing them all to achieve happiness and fulfillment. Our physical health is intimately linked with our mental health. And once you improve your mental health and happiness, your physical health will also improve. The goal is to inspire you to make a change in your life by focusing on improving your mental health so that you can achieve the lifestyle of your dreams.

2.   Do you feel overwhelmed by stress and anxiety?

If you feel overwhelmed by stress and anxiety, it's time to take a step back and evaluate your life. Our lives are full of responsibilities and obligations, which can be good, but only if we can handle them. There is no need to blame other people for our problems. But instead, focus on the things we can change in ourselves. The first step is to understand ourselves better. We have all heard that we must 'do what makes us happy.' But how do we tell what will make us happy? This book will help you answer this question by helping you find happiness first in your mental health.

3.   Are you feeling depressed, or do you have anxiety?

Depression and anxiety are common issues that people face, but they don't have to control your life or define you and your abilities. Are you ready to take action to make a change in your life and live happier? If the answer is yes, then this book is for you!

4. Do you find your thoughts run 100 miles per hour?

Do you overanalyze things to find adverse outcomes? Are you overthinking situations and speculating about negative consequences? Do you make mountains out of molehills at times? I will share with you some ways to declutter the mind and have peaceful thoughts that works with the present, not the past or speculation of the future.

5. Are you searching for your true self: your own set of values and goals in life?

There's a winner inside all of us, but sometimes we need to find a way to help that person win. Think about it. What differentiates us from everyone else? Do you have a whole set of values and goals you have never thought about? Maybe your mind has been programmed to believe that you need more money, more things, or a certain status. But perhaps it's time for a change of mind.

6. Are you searching for meaning in your life?

    People often search for a purpose in their lives. They ask, 'why am I here?' or 'what am I meant to be doing with my life?' We live our lives based on what other people or our environment thinks we should be doing. We don't know why we are here, but those who do know have discovered the answer and are determined to maintain it! That can be you.

7. Are you tired of the same old routine and want a change in life direction?

    Familiarity can breed contempt, and while familiarity might not be too bad in moderation, it can become very unhealthy in the long term. Do you find yourself wedged in a rut? Are you looking for ways to change your life?

8. Are you so far down the rabbit hole that you don't know how you will live your entire life this way?

    I am not a psychotherapist; even if I were, a book does not replace therapy. Some of you will learn that therapy is a better approach for you than the advice I have to offer. If that's you, I do plan on helping you make that decision, and what you learn here will be supplementary to your growth with your therapist.

9. Are you concerned about the mental health of your children or someone close to you?

    You can have exceptional mental health but have a family member or close friend who doesn't, and you want to learn more so you can help. If that is the case, good for you for taking up this challenge. This book is also for you.

What we need on our journey to better health and happiness is to be able to accept ourselves the way we are now, not where we will be after we have completed our journey. We need to choose happiness and fulfillment in our lives today because they will give us the strength to continue that journey. Perhaps you've never been one who could say, 'I'm happy with myself.' If this is you, I want you to know that you can achieve a happier life! It may seem like an insurmountable obstacle, but if each day of your life starts by saying, 'I am happy today' or 'I am happy with my life,' then you'll begin to see a change in your attitude on life.

Every word you say to yourself plants a seed of truth and behavior in your subconscious mind, so remember Marisa Peer's quote:

"The most important words you will ever hear are the words you say to yourself. So, make them positive. Make them kind."

This is the first step in changing your mind.

Introduction

Many of us are familiar with the famous quote by Albert Einstein: 'No problem can be solved by the same level of consciousness that created it.' This is because bringing about lasting change requires a different approach and state of mind. Have you heard the definition of insanity? 'Doing the same thing repeatedly and expecting the result to improve.'

In other words, to have a different, more desirable outcome requires you to become the change you want to see in the world. The happier and healthier we become, the better our minds will function – allowing us to achieve more in our lives.

Isn't it interesting that Albert Einstein, teacher, philosopher, Theoretical Physicist, and inventor of the world-renowned General Theory of Relativity, would recognize this fundamental principle of how our world and within it, we human beings operate?

Our minds, consciousness, and thoughts are the creators of our reality. They are the energy architects of everything we experience, including our mental health. Herein lies the power that we all inherently possess. As many people have already discovered to their benefit, becoming peaceful, calm, and centered in your mind is a powerful secret behind bringing about positive change in your life. It is also one of the most effective tools for reversing and overcoming severe emotional issues such as depression, anxiety, fear, stress, and other negative emotions.

The Hedonic Treadmill

Modern society has conditioned us to believe that we need to have all the material things in life before we can be happy and that our happiness will come after achieving some goal. I assure you there is no benefit to waiting for something to be perfect in your life before you decide to be happy. If this is your plan, things may never be perfect, so you may never be satisfied. There is no reason to wait to decide to be happy.

Consumerism, the belief that we will climb higher and higher in life if we buy more and more, has taught us to believe things before looking at ourselves.

But if you look closely at this, you'll see how it works. You'll be told that you need to achieve a goal to be happy, and then when you reach the destination, your happiness only lasts for a short time until another goal pops up and causes stress or worry. This is an endless cycle.

It is only when we look inside ourselves, consciously and with an open mind, to discover what we might have believed all along is not valid and that we can begin to change our lives for the better.

This book will guide you on a journey of self-discovery and help you realize what it means to be 'happy' – not just today but within yourself. And how to use this knowledge to bring happiness and fulfillment in your life. To become content and happy beyond your achievements or belongings.

Our mental well-being and happiness do not depend on what we achieve in life. It's the other way around! The more we allow ourselves to be happy and free from stress and anxiety, the better we will be equipped to achieve our goals. To be productive and creative and to live in balance and harmony, we must look after our minds.

Mental Health

A Prerequisite to Success?

Chapter 1

There seems to be no clear consensus about the definition of mental health. Words like 'well-being,' 'happiness,' 'fulfillment,' and 'positive emotions' are often used interchangeably. If we base our definition of mental health on happiness alone (which is an excellent place to start), we will discover that it means far more than feeling good from time to time. It means feeling calm, cheerful, and peaceful most of the time, regardless of the circumstances or our current mental state.

Determining the true meaning of mental health has been the subject of many debates among philosophers throughout history. To Plato, it meant *"inner harmony and peace of mind, which is free from worry, fear or anger."* To Aristotle, it meant being *"comfortable with yourself and the world."*

Ancient Eastern cultures have consistently recognized mental health as the state of being at peace within oneself. Mentally healthy people are happy with themselves, and they accept their imperfections. They do not need to prove anything to anyone else to validate themselves, and they find it easy to give without expecting anything in return.

A mentally healthy person has an even temper, enthusiasm for living, a sense of humor, and curiosity about life. When a person is in mental balance, these qualities are all present in their life.

In the 18th century, Dr. Benjamin Rush, a psychiatrist who was the mental health father, proposed that mental illnesses were physical diseases. This idea opposed the notion that mental illnesses were caused by demonic possession. Rush believed that conditions of the mind were treatable through moral therapy, which consisted of prayer, self-examination, and work.

In the 20th century, the Mental Health Movement was born. The idea of 'mental hygiene' became a primary focus of reform efforts, with figures like Clifford Wight, who said that all people must uphold their *'duty to preserve and enhance their mental health.'* This new focus on mental health came when society began to take notice of the need for medical services which would treat the mentally ill rather than confining them in jails or asylums.

Today, we know that mental health disorders result from chemical imbalances within the brain and that these symptoms can be effectively treated with psychotherapy and medications.

What is Mental Health?

Mental health is about the state of mind, a continuum from mild stress to mental illness. Mental health refers to a person's ability to function in their life. It embodies our ability to enjoy the external world and ourselves without fear. Mental health disorders affect our thinking, behavior, emotions, relationships, and overall well-being.

The Big Picture

Our mental health is just one of the five facets of our well-being that affect us daily. These five areas are physical, emotional, mental, social, and financial health. An individual's well-being is also affected by their life circumstances, such as relationships with family, friends, and co-workers, as well as the stress level in the workplace. Whether we experience these influences for good or bad depends on how we deal with them. It is our choice how they will affect us.

Physical Health

Our mental health impacts our physical health; you cannot be happy and mentally healthy without good physical health. Our overall well-being depends on a well-balanced diet, regular physical exercise, mental health,[6] and adequate sleep. Our mental health can affect our physical health in the long term because our mental state may influence our level of stress or the risk of illness. Mental disorders such as depression can cause much stress to the body. This can lead to heart problems and high blood pressure, which is unhealthy for both body and mind.

Exercising can also help boost our physical health. The endorphins released in the brain during and after exercise can improve our mood and make us happier. We may also gain a better sense of self-worth from being able to take care of our bodies regularly.

I recommend getting the following weekly exercise to support the body and mind. If you can't get here overnight, that is okay. Start implementing some of each of these four building blocks of exercise:

- Strength Training: Two 30-minute sessions a week at least 48 hours apart, one working the upper body and the other the lower body.
- Zone 2 Training: This zone is about getting your heart rate to 60-70% of its maximum (max). Your max heart rate is 220 minus your age. Ideally, you complete four

45-minute sessions weekly. You can do this on a treadmill, brisk walking, playing tennis or pickleball, or whatever gets your heart rate into zone 2.

- Zone 5 Training: This zone is about getting your heart rate to 90-100% of its max. Don't worry; you don't need to be here for very long. Ideally, you reach your zone 5 heart rate and stay there for four minutes, followed by four minutes of recovery. Repeat five times. If you've not done zone 5 training before, you can start with one minute in zone 5 and two minutes in recovery.
- Stability Exercises: A Yoga or Pilates class is ideal once weekly, but you can also complete some stability exercises on your own such as one-legged stance, tree pose, etc.

As you grow older, keeping physically fit becomes more critical to your overall health because it helps you to remain active, mobile, and independent. In my book, Longevity Secrets, released in late 2022, I review these exercises in more detail.

Emotional Health

Emotional health encompasses an individual's feelings and relationships with others. Mental disorders such as depression can cause significant pain to the individual; for this reason, physical and emotional health is about balance. For a person to be emotionally healthy, they must be filled with positive emotions instead of negative ones.

Difficulties at home or work that prevent us from creating a happy environment can lead to mental illness. How we deal with these problems sets the pace for our emotional stability. For example, if we have much stress at home, but can manage it positively, such as by talking about it with our family and friends, we will be less likely to develop mental health disorders.

If we suffer from emotional distress due to life circumstances such as losing a job or breaking up with a partner, the best way to get out of this rut is by taking action in other parts of our lives. The sense of accomplishment gained from solving our issues can give us the emotional strength to face future challenges in life.

Financial Health

Our financial health is all about living according to our means while providing for ourselves and those we care about financially. People with positive financial health are generally relaxed about money and do not worry about their future. They are also confident they can deal with life's unexpected challenges. A sound financial foundation also plays an essential role in developing good mental health by helping us face our difficulties and conquer them instead of avoiding or hiding them.

The peace of mind that comes with financial security is good for our mental health and makes it easier to deal with any problems. When life throws a curveball at these individuals who have no problem spending wisely and saving correctly, they are less likely to develop mental health disorders.

Social Health

Your social health refers to how you relate to others and how others relate to you. It is about your relationships with your friends and family members and how much you feel supported by those around you. These relationships give us emotional strength to deal with difficult times, especially during physical or emotional illnesses that can occur at any point.

Friends and family are important sources of emotional support since they understand you and the issues you are dealing with in your life. Healthcare professionals also can be of great help if we suffer from a mental health disorder. Knowing that you are not alone, whether you feel happy or sad, is essential.

The way you deal with difficult life circumstances significantly affects your social health. For example, when people feel like their lives are full of good relationships, they will probably cope better with any emotional issues or mental illnesses by seeking the support of family and friends. If a person does not have many close relationships, they may find it more challenging to handle the stress, leading to mental disorders such as depression.

Common Mental Disorders and What Causes Them

When hearing about mental health, we tend to think of 'serious' mental conditions like schizophrenia or bipolar while ignoring the more common disorders caused by issues that are not as serious such as an unhealthy environment, daily stress, or life circumstances. These conditions can still be harmful, though less threatening in the way schizophrenia and other more severe conditions are. In this section, we'll look at some of the more common disorders that most of us will experience at some point in our lives, what causes them and what we can do about them.

Anxiety

Anxiety is a feeling of fear and dread that can manifest in many forms. It may be experienced physically (for example, a rapid heartbeat), mentally (constant worrying), or behavioral (avoiding an activity). Although anxiety has many possible causes and symptoms, it is generally described as the feelings of fear, nervousness, and worry that often occur with depression. Anxiety is an adverse reaction that can lead to much more severe issues.

What Causes Anxiety?

Anxiety disorders are caused by the over-activation of the body's fear and stress response system. This means that when the body is exposed to a harmful stimulus, such as a loud noise or an impending accident, it reacts by increasing the activity of the stress system. This can result in unpleasant symptoms such as rapid heartbeat, shaking, and sweating.

When we are anxious, our body's stress response system goes into overdrive. Think of it as a mechanism to alert us to potentially harmful stimuli. If we feel threatened when we haven't experienced it, our body will naturally activate the stress response system to ensure our well-being.

How to cope with anxiety?

The best way to overcome anxiety is by learning how to control or change how we react to uncertain situations. If you feel anxious, try not to focus on what may occur but instead concentrate on how you will respond to the problem using your cognitive and behavioral skills. By practicing these skills regularly, you can train yourself so that your body and mind will automatically react more wisely.

Distraction and relaxation techniques can be beneficial in controlling the anxiety that is caused by the stress response system. Some practical techniques include breathing exercises, meditation, muscle relaxation, and visualization.

Mood Disorders

Mood disorders cover many mental health problems characterized by persistent mood changes. People with depression and bipolar disorder suffer from a distinct difference in their mood, often referred to as affect. Symptoms of depression include thoughts of self-harm, feelings of sadness, and loss of interest in pleasurable activities. Other symptoms may include reduced energy levels and appetite, headaches, irritability, social withdrawal, and insomnia.

Mood swings are usually characteristic of bipolar disorder. A person with this condition goes through periods where their mood is depressed or elevated. People suffering from either depression or bipolar disorder may experience extreme forms of these emotions that interfere with their daily lives. Medical interventions may be necessary. However, the information we are discussing can also help but may not be the only therapy needed to manage these disorders.

What causes mood disorders?

The exact cause of mood disorders is unknown, but several factors, including mental health conditions, brain structure abnormalities, diet, exercise, and genetics, have been likely to contribute. There are even studies that support the health of the gut affecting the health of the brain.[2]

These conditions are often related to neurotransmitters. Neurotransmitters are chemical message carriers. They carry messages between nerve cells. When a nerve cell is stimulated, neurotransmitters are released into the space between neurons and attach to receptors on other cells, thereby transmitting signals. Some of these transmitters include dopamine, serotonin, and adrenaline.

In mood disorders, neurotransmitters in the stress response system are probably abnormally regulated. The levels of these transmitters may be either too low or too high. What is certain is that having too much of any one transmitter can cause harmful effects on another part of the body and brain function.

Eating Disorders

Common eating disorders include anorexia nervosa, bulimia nervosa, and binge eating disorder. There is even a night eating disorder.

Eating disorders cause significant distress to those suffering from them and their family. This leads to people engaging in dangerous behavior such as fasting or purging and may also have suicidal thoughts. Eating disorders are associated with various life difficulties, including low self-esteem, poor body image, and social isolation. These issues can often be resolved through therapy and effective medications.

Personality Disorder

Mental health conditions involve abnormal behavior and attitudes that often are not logical and cannot be explained. For example, obsessive-compulsive disorder (OCD) is a type of personality disorder where the person suffers from specific obsessions and compulsions that cause distress and limit their life. Personality disorders may be present from birth but often develop in adolescence or early adulthood.

Personality disorders may influence people's perception of themselves, others, and the world. This may lead to a negative self-image, poor social skills, and avoiding contact with others.

A personality disorder may be treated with a combination of medication and professional therapy and is outside the scope of this book. A person being treated for a personality disorder might need support to reduce the risks that a personality clash could cause. For example, suppose an outgoing person has been diagnosed with an avoidant personality disorder. In that case, they might need support to help them make social connections and to overcome their fear of rejection.

Why Mental Well-being is Important

Mental health is a universal concern and can be best described as 'being in harmony with one's emotions, thoughts, and values.' Mental health is not a sickness but rather a state of being. It is a measure of how well we are either functioning or malfunctioning. Mental well-being is the degree to which we can function optimally. It is our ability to experience pleasure, cope with challenges, and live life according to our standards. Here's why mental health is so important.

A Natural Expression of Emotions

Many people consider it a sign of weakness to show their feelings or allow themselves to be vulnerable. However, it is only through expressing our emotions that we can comprehend and learn from them. It's okay to be angry, it's okay to be sad, and most importantly, it's okay to let others see those emotions. Expressing your feelings isn't a sign of weakness; it's a sign of strength.

When you recognize and express your emotions, you can better understand yourself and those around you. It allows you to interact with others and the world more maturely.

Experience Pleasure

The ability to be happy is crucial for mental health. When you are happy, your mind becomes more creative, your body heals faster, and you have access to a more accurate memory of events through the happiness that comes with living life in the present moment. You can also think of ways to improve happiness for yourself or others. When you're experiencing pleasure, there's no room for fear or self-doubt.

Your Ability to Cope

Your environment influences you; whether you like it or not, something always occurs at every moment that affects you. Having sound mental health allows you to deal with these issues more effectively and, in turn, helps you live a better quality of life and enjoy people and experiences more fully.

Challenges are part of life, and having sound mental health allows you to cope with them better. When you become trapped in a cycle of anxiety and depression, the situation often becomes more complex than you can manage on your own. The better your mental health is, the more you can face life's challenges and see how you deal with them.

You Can Take Responsibility

Life is full of opportunities to make changes that improve our lives and the lives of others around us. We often put our happiness in other people's hands and expect them to make us feel happy, which can lead to frustration or helplessness. It's empowering to take responsibility for your own life and a sign of maturity to take responsibility for the lives of others.

Nothing will ever be perfect, but you can make your life as happy as it can be. If you are unhappy with something, change how you feel so that you may see a change in your situation. I realize that is easier said than done, but I am here to help you learn how.

Our Mental Well Being

The Connection Between Mental Health and Overall Health

Chapter 2

Mental health is defined as a state of psychological well-being, and mental illness is a state of psychological ill-health. Mental health has many different interpretations, but generally, it is understood to refer to our emotional and psychological functioning. This can include how we think, how we act, how we feel and how we deal with life in general. A person's mental health may affect their behavior or the way they think at any given time, and being 'mentally healthy' is the same as being 'mentally well.'

The way that our brain functions may be influenced by our genes or by factors in the environment. Things that happen to us or around us, as well as all our life experiences and thoughts, can affect our feelings, beliefs, and behaviors.

'Mind Over Matter' is a phrase I'm sure you have heard before. It's the idea that our minds are more powerful than circumstances. Some also relate it to our physical health, indicating that our minds have incredible power over our bodies; if our minds aren't healthy, our bodies can't be healthy.

Our minds have a much stronger influence over us than most people can imagine. Mental Health issues like anxiety and depression can often be linked to physical ailments. It's common for people with high levels of stress to be diagnosed with chronic illnesses like heart disease, respiratory problems, and cancer. Our minds can help us live longer as well. People with positive attitudes are more likely to take better care of themselves and be more active, leading to a healthier body overall. It's also common for people suffering from anxiety and depression to engage in unhealthy behaviors such as smoking or drinking alcohol excessively.

Stress does a lot to our bodies; it can cause us to feel like we have no control over the situation and cannot handle what is happening. Even if the stressor isn't huge or something has already happened, sometimes we don't know how to deal with it or let it go. We might not know what to do or what would make us feel better at the time. Anxiety and depression are linked to stress because they often come from some difficulty in life that triggers stress reactions in our bodies and minds. But they are different because they manifest differently in other people and situations.

Anxiety causes physical tension in our muscles which causes much discomfort. If we keep worrying about the situation or something going wrong, our bodies start to shut down. We can feel like we are not in control of ourselves and that our mind is elsewhere.

Where Mental Health Issues Originate

We could blame factors beyond our control, like our genetics, for our mental health, but the reality is that we're just as responsible for our mental health as we are for our physical health. I'm talking about our choices and actions. Factors beyond our control, like genetics, may contribute to an issue. However, in the end, we're still responsible for our thoughts and for taking action to get help when needed and making the necessary lifestyle changes.

Let us consider depression, for example. Lacking purpose in life or being content is undoubtedly a factor contributing to depression. If we feel we have no purpose in life, versus if we decide that we can determine our purpose, those are choices we make that will dramatically affect our happiness in life. Most of our happiness comes down to our own decisions and actions.

The power of choice is a fantastic thing. We can choose how we want to respond to the daily stresses in life through our actions. When you're facing a difficult situation that could lead you into depression or another mental health issue, act by confronting it head-on instead of trying to ignore it and pretending it doesn't exist. It's essential to be aware of our mindset or attitude. A positive attitude will help you solve problems. The mental health issues that we struggle with are not impossible to overcome, but they will require action on our part. We'll have to make changes to the way that we think and act. Sometimes these changes can be gradual, but they may require a dramatic lifestyle change.

The Dangers of Poor Mental Health

Hopefully, by now, you can agree that our mental health is ultimately up to us. We must realize how important it is to take responsibility for our health and well-being. When we don't make the necessary changes to help ourselves, there will be negative consequences, and the outcome is almost always negative.

When you don't take control of your mental health and continue a destructive path, you may find yourself isolated from friends or family members. In this way, people suffering from depression may cut themselves off from the only people they can turn to for help. Here are a few adverse outcomes associated with poor mental health:

Isolation from Loved Ones

When going through a difficult time, it's common for us to want to isolate ourselves from other people. We get stuck in a negative cycle of self-doubt and self-pity. This can lead to many deteriorating relationships.

With low self-esteem, we start to believe that we are not good enough or worthy of being liked by others. This can lead to feelings of inner emptiness and struggles with self-image, confidence, and motivation. When facing a life-threatening illness or struggling with depression, these feelings can sometimes be overwhelming and cause us to feel worthless.

Loss of Employment or Career Opportunity

We may take much longer to finish a project when we're stressed or demotivated. Over time this will begin to harm our work performance, and we can lose our job. When we're depressed or anxious, we may not be able to perform at our best, which will start to show in our work.

Relationship Challenges

Many people with mental health concerns cannot find a way to express their feelings and emotions, resulting in them becoming bitter and resentful towards those around them. A person suffering from depression can become disconnected from those they love and unable to trust anyone with their emotions. This can result in challenges in being unable to communicate with others, leading to the deterioration of close relationships.

It's hard to enjoy friendships or romantic relationships when our thinking is so clouded. You might feel like you're not in control of your life and powerless, which is not how you should feel. If you know someone struggling with some mental health issue, be there for them like they are there for you when you need them the most.

Increased Chance of Drug or Alcohol Abuse

There is a direct link between drug and alcohol abuse and poor mental health. Many people with anxiety and depression turn to drugs or alcohol to self-medicate. This is an unhealthy way of dealing with mental health issues. Still, unfortunately, it's widespread because it helps people escape their problems temporarily and forget about the pain they're feeling.

Financial Stress

Financial stress can be a result or a symptom of poor mental health. If you're struggling with poor mental health, you may be demotivated and even not make it to work. You might not accept a promotion due to the fear of failure, or you may have opportunities to earn more that you don't take. This can result in financial stress.

Additionally, financial issues for other reasons can cause quite a bit of stress and result in poor mental health. Undoubtedly, it is easier to have positive, empowering thoughts without financial stress.

When people feel depressed and hopeless about their life, suicide can seem like the only way out. If we're not careful, this desperation feeling can start taking on a life of its own and begin to control our lives. This is when it becomes essential that we take action to deal with our mental health issues and work at finding a solution or treatment plan.

There's always hope.

Ways of Taking Care of Your Mental Well-Being

Feeling good about one's life is easier said than done for most of us. I'm addressing this now. Let's learn how we can take care of our mental well-being and feel better about our lives by consciously choosing to do so. The opposite of happiness isn't sadness; it's indifference. That is always a choice. We all can be happy and joyful. It's simply a question of whether we choose to or not.

Sleep

Yes, there is a connection between sleep and our mental health. If there were one thing that most could do immediately to impact mental health positively, it would be an improvement in the quality and quantity of our sleep.

Sleep does wonders for our mental health. First, it helps to prevent depression. If you don't get enough quality natural sleep, you can start to feel hopeless and despairing because your brain didn't get enough time to process the events of the day and prepare for the next day. Sleep deprivation is also a significant factor in anxiety and panic attacks since it increases the reactions in portions of the brain linked with anxiety.[24]

As well as preventing anxiety, sleep gives us the energy to be happier. Lack of sleep causes decreased activity in some parts of the brain and leaves us feeling exhausted, unmotivated, and lacking any interest in doing anything productive with our day. When we are awake for too long, we use our ability to concentrate on one thing and then begin to feel scattered with too many thoughts on one topic floating around in our minds.

Quality natural sleep allows our bodies and minds to repair and detoxify so that we can function better when we are awake. If you are tired, you will be cranky, irritable, and not fun to be around. And if this is a chronic condition, your mental and physical health will certainly suffer.

Nutrition

Eating well and having a healthy lifestyle are important aspects of maintaining mental health. There are plenty of ways to eat more nutritious, such as cutting down on processed foods, choosing more whole foods, and eating fewer animal products. Doing so will help your immune system, give you the energy you need to do the things you love, and most importantly, make you feel better about yourself.

One way you can start your path towards eating better is by making it easier for yourself when you're hungry by keeping healthy snacks. Maintaining healthy snack foods in your home is essential to avoid being tempted by the luxury of unhealthy foods.

Relaxation

Pamper yourself for no other reason than because you deserve it. Be kind to yourself throughout the day and focus on things that make you happy. What makes you happy might be watching a comedy show, listening to music, reading a book, drawing, walking, or taking a nap. It doesn't matter what you choose if it's something that makes you feel better, doesn't hurt others, isn't unhealthy, and when you do it, your mood improves.

State of Mind

It is easy to focus on the negative when we live our entire lives within the winter of our heads. There will be a storm in the future, but this does not mean that all possibilities of rain, snow, or sun will follow suit.

There are positives about everything: it's good for us to see this and remember how fortunate we are to be alive, to have our family and health. If it rains all day, and it was the day you planned on running a 5k, instead of being upset that your run was canceled, remember all the good rain does for the earth. Use it as an opportunity to read a good book. Or find another way to make good use of the rain shower.

A positive outlook in life is essential. It's good to be positive, but at the same time, it's ok to have a sense of melancholy and sorrow. We are not always going to feel happy all the time. Go with the flow and try your best to find something good whenever you can.

When an unfortunate event happens, choose to learn from your mistakes, if applicable, instead of beating yourself up. Beating yourself up does not help you grow. Learn from your mistakes and become a better version of yourself.

When you make a mistake, you need to allow yourself to accept that it happened and then move on from there. Everyone makes mistakes. None of us are perfect. Mistakes or failures are an opportunity to learn and grow; it's also an opportunity to develop your sense of humor. Laugh at yourself and know what to do next time, and move on.

Moving on from an unfortunate event does not mean that you should forget about it; it just means that there's nothing more we can do except learn to avoid making the same mistake again. Get rid of any guilt and shame you feel about your past because you can't change it. You can only change the future.

You must realize that your past influenced whom you have become, but it never determines whom you will become. What occurs in the future will have a more significant influence on whom you will become. And it's your choices that will make all the difference.

Finding the positive in everything is a learned skill, and much of the balance of this book will show you ways you can find something to be happy about every day. You can choose ways to avoid stress and gain joy; avoid depression and find self-worth; avoid anxiety and gain pleasure.

You can take steps towards improving mental health by consciously choosing to do so. If you can't implement everything I'm sharing today, that's ok. You can make minor improvements over time. It's important not to pressure yourself into having to change everything overnight. Do things one step at a time, and be sure you're doing something best for your happiness and well-being before anything else.

Overthinking

Chapter 3

We've all been through it before. Someone says something, and you know you should say 'ok' or 'sure, why not?' But instead, your mind gives you a thousand reasons why you should ask them questions, try to work out their intentions, or even remind them of promises they made that conflict with what they're saying now.

People who overthink everything tend to question the true intentions of others and think that they can predict the future of every situation. Overthinking can make us cautious of what other people think of us because we will may be thinking about their expectations of us and how we should meet them, do they have a hidden agenda or what we believe they're not saying. Sometimes this overthinking can even lead to a 'worrying about our worry' effect, where we worry about whether we should worry in the first place.

So many thoughts are going on, causing stress. If you find this happening, it's time to declutter the mind. Often, this internal questioning to find hypothetical answers creates emotions that aren't necessary and often aren't relevant.

Overthinking is a common challenge and can arise from several different things: having a lot on your plate at work, low self-esteem causing you to worry too much about other people's opinions, a subconscious behavior learned from one of your parents or siblings, or just being over-analytical in general. Some people can't be happy unless everything around them is perfect. Whatever causes us to overthink and overanalyze things, it's essential to learn how to look at situations differently to prevent ourselves from overthinking when it's not necessary and, therefore, better control our emotions.

It's time to learn how to control emotions so that you are less likely to overthink and cause unnecessary stress in the future. I'll also give you some tips on how to manage your time better, learn how to be more flexible, and accept things that may have been difficult to accept in the past. Moreover, I will share some examples of what overthinking might sound like and discuss why it should be avoided.

When the Mind Goes on Overdrive

In this example, overthinking is when we focus too much on negative possibilities, the worst that can happen, and the downside of situations instead of focusing on the current situation and the positive aspects of what could happen, which can be more probable and more likely to be true. When overthinking, our thoughts don't focus on solving whatever problem we're thinking about. Instead, our thoughts will often go over and over in our minds, reflecting on what happened in the past, speculating whether it would happen again in the future, and wondering why things are not happening as planned.

The fact that we experience these thoughts can often be attributed to being too analytical or looking at every situation from an opposing viewpoint, even when there are no good reasons for doing so. Because we are thinking about potential problems before they even happen, it's effortless for us to fear what might happen if things go wrong. In essence, we are creating an adverse outcome in our minds and suffering the feelings associated with it before it ever happens. And often, it never happens. There is no benefit from suffering these negative emotions over something that hasn't happened and may never will.

Catastrophizing and
The Imposter Syndrome

A classic case of overthinking is catastrophizing. This is when we assume things are much worse than they are, even when there is no evidence. Have you heard the phrase making a mountain out of a molehill? That is catastrophizing a molehill indeed. Often when people catastrophize, it's more about how they feel at that moment than the actual situation. Have you ever noticed that making a mountain out of a molehill is more about everything else that went on that day? Or, more to the point that you're stressed or have anxiety for some reason when this occurs.

Imposter syndrome is feeling inadequate despite evidence of skill and success. It's when you doubt your capabilities and feel like you're a fraud. For example, if you were a successful sales manager in others' eyes, but you can't see it yourself, you feel like you're only playing the role and aren't as good as they say you are or as your results show you to be. Although many people experience this sensation from time to time, some have this feeling more often than others. When we have imposter syndrome, we focus on our failures and imperfections without giving credit to our successes. It's directly related to self-esteem.

Catastrophizing and imposter syndrome are the two biggest culprits when overthinking. The way to avoid them is by changing the way you think about yourself and the situations that you are in. Rather than thinking about how things could go wrong, it would be best if you focused on how things could go right. Instead of focusing on mistakes or failures, you must see them as learning opportunities and focus on successes.

I know it's easier said than done, but you must begin to try. Consider that overthinking in this manner typically occurs when you are feeling anxious or stressed. Managing anxiety and stress is the first step to stopping to overthink. But also working on your self-esteem will help too. You are valuable and worthy, and you must believe in yourself.

By knowing yourself and accepting yourself as worthy, you can create a positive self-image that will help to keep you from overthinking. The more confident you are in your ability to complete tasks and the more comfortable you are with who you are as a person, the less likely you will worry about how others perceive you, and this will help you avoid overthinking.

A mentor of mine in my early career days, Tom Hopkins, a sales trainer, says, "fake it until you make it."[10] This philosophy of his was directly related to being good at sales. However, I like to incorporate it into much of life. For example, as it relates to overthinking, if you have low self-esteem, pretend that you don't. Pretend to be a person with high self-esteem. How would that person act? And then play that part. If you play the role of someone with high self-esteem, it's only a matter of time before your subconscious mind will believe you have high self-esteem.

I work with many overweight and obese patients. Similarly, if they can start acting like a thin person, it will only be a matter of time before they become thin.

These are examples of "faking it until you make it" and can easily be used to combat imposter syndrome and catastrophizing.

By convincing your subconscious mind through your actions that you have high self-esteem, for example, you will develop it. This approach can be taken with many things. When it comes to overthinking, doubting yourself will make things worse. If you feel insecure about how you're doing at work or school, you might worry about whether people will like you because of your performance. None of this is helpful.

This is a negative cycle. When you are worried about how others will perceive you, this worry can affect your performance, affecting your self-esteem. If you don't feel good about yourself, you might begin worrying that people think you're not good at something or can't do it well. A negative perception of yourself might cause you to overthink how others feel about you. This spirals out of control until it causes needless stress and anxiety over something that isn't reality and may never even happen.

Instead, you can play the role of someone with a lot of confidence and someone who's famous. Your subconscious mind doesn't know the difference between fiction and reality, so playing the role of someone with the characteristics you'd like to develop will help you develop those characteristics.

The "fake it until you make it" attitude creates a mindset that you are already an expert. When I was in my late 20s, a few of us at work decided to go skydiving. It was a tandem jump, meaning I was attached to another experienced jumpmaster. But initially, I began to overthink what could happen. I certainly was more scared about doing this than I had been about anything in life. But I took on this "fake it until I make it" attitude and kept telling myself that this was no big deal. I faked that I wasn't afraid. I found some facts that showed how safe tandem jumps were and kept convincing myself through my positive self-talk that I could do this. So many others had. Some of my coworkers were going to do it, and so can I. I told myself repeatedly that this would be fun and something I would happily remember for the rest of my life. I pretended that I had no fear and that this would be fun.

As you might have guessed, I did complete the jump, and if it weren't for my positive self-talk, avoiding negative overthinking and fake it until I make it attitude, I might not have been able to do so. I share this because I learned such a valuable lesson. Not only did I prove that positive self-talk works, but I also learned that if you do what you fear, you overcome fear.

Dwelling on the Past

Another example of overthinking would be when we dwell on the past. In this situation, we worry about something that has already happened, even though there's nothing we can do to change the past. We're still thinking about how bad it was. Some people will even go as far as obsessing over what might have happened if something had been done differently. This type of thinking is not constructive.

The critical thing to remember is that there is no use dwelling on events that have already happened because you cannot change the past. The only thing you can do is learn from your mistakes and make sure that they don't happen in the future so that they don't affect other aspects of your life.

If the adverse situation in the past has nothing to do with your mistakes, then attempt to find a way to learn from it regardless. The more we realize the good that comes from bad situations, the easier it is to let go of the past and accept future things that don't go your way.

When you live in the past, you forego the present and live in an imaginary future, which you should avoid at all costs. The past is over, and the present and future are what matter. If you spend more time looking at the past than the future, it teaches your subconscious mind to allow your mind to dwell on things that have already occurred. We don't want to create a habit of dwelling on the past.

When you think about the past or how things could have been different, without realizing it, you're letting your mind lose focus on what's essential. Overthinking can become a problem because of this. It would be best if you learned how to put yourself in the moment so that your thoughts do not go back into the past or into a life that does not exist anymore.

One way to ensure that this doesn't happen is to avoid making things worse than they are. Rather than thinking about why things are going wrong, it's better to focus on why they can go right and find solutions rather than dwelling on events that have already happened.

Let's say you fought with your partner, and you're thinking about why it happened and how it could have been avoided. If you performed poorly in an exam, you might wonder why you failed and how things could have gone differently.

These thoughts can be helpful, but only if you learn from them and move on. Obsessing these thoughts is very destructive in preventing you from moving forward with your life. If this continues, it becomes a vicious cycle where your thoughts are focused on how you could have done better instead of how well you are doing now.

The key lesson here is to learn from the past but never live there. Learning from the past is the goal. Wishing you had a life as if the past were different is not and is harmful to your mental health.

Focus on the present and think about what your next course of action is going to be. If things are not going well, try to determine why. Evaluate why things are not going how you would like and change your ways to get back on track. Remember, you cannot change others; you can only change yourself. So, ask yourself what you will do next time and then act in that direction to improve the results for the future.

When we make a mistake, it doesn't mean that we're failures or not worth being around. It just means we made a mistake, and now we can learn from it so that it doesn't happen again. No one is perfect. No one. It is okay if you're not perfect, either. No one expects perfection from you, and you do not need to expect it from yourself or others.

Accepting Uncertainty

The fear of the unknown is a typical case of overthinking. When we don't know what to expect, our minds begin to imagine all sorts of undesirable outcomes.

Therefore, it's essential to learn how to accept uncertainty. The more comfortable we are with ambiguity and not knowing, the less likely we will overthink things we don't understand or can't explain. Anticipating problems before they happen is a typical case of overthinking. It can be very harmful because it keeps our minds busy with negative thoughts instead of focusing on what's essential in life. This can result in you thinking about why something might not work out in the future rather than accepting that you cannot control how things will happen. You will be happier if you anticipate desirable outcomes instead of anticipating problems.

As soon as these negative thoughts enter your mind, change them to positive ones. This will take a conscious effort, but if negativity enters your thoughts, replace it with a positive outcome, let it go out of your mind, and move on to something else.

When we dwell on things outside our control, like stormy weather, we're just adding more negative thoughts to our minds, which is not productive. It's crucial to accept uncertainty when you don't have all the pieces of the puzzle together, and you shouldn't beat yourself up thinking about things that might never happen.

I have Crohn's disease and, for a myriad of reasons, found myself in the hospital in April of 2022 with an abscess in my colon. I had a tennis ball size mass developing in my sigmoid colon, and I was admitted so they could attempt to drain the abscess.

After five days in the hospital, as the abscess was being successfully drained, my colon ruptured, and I had feces leaking out of my body where the drain had been inserted. The doctors anticipated that even if we drained the abscess successfully, my colon would not be able to heal. Therefore, I had scheduled a colectomy, the removal of my colon, for the Tuesday following. But now the colectomy surgery needed to occur urgently. The surgery was moved up to just hours after the colon ruptured, and what used to be a very low-risk surgery now had significant risk.

The colectomy scheduled a few days out was going to be planned well. I would have cleansed the colon, like when you prepare for a colonoscopy, to ensure bacteria and other harmful matter wouldn't have access to the inside of my body. And for that reason, the risks associated with the surgery were very low.

But now, none of the preparation could be done and what should have been only an hour to hour and a half surgery became a three-and-a-half-hour surgery because of all the cleanup that had to occur. The risk associated with fatality increased, and the risk of infection was almost inevitable.

Of course, I immediately began to think negative thoughts. I began to hypothesize what could happen; every outcome I was thinking about was negative. There's no doubt that the first thought I had was that I wasn't prepared to die. I blamed my gastroenterologist for taking me off some meds that kept my symptoms at bay and putting me on a biologic, which my body ultimately developed antibodies against. All the negative thoughts of blame and fear instantly occurred. But I realized that the outcome was out of my control, and I quickly decided that I needed to reset my thoughts.

I explained to myself that it wasn't Dr. Schmitz's fault. He was trying to help me by putting me on a biologic based on the chronic deep ulcers I had developed over the years of having Crohn's. It was only a matter of time before I was going to lose my colon without biological therapy. The fact that the rupture occurred while I was in the hospital getting my abscess drained is a blessing. I might not have even realized that it ruptured if they didn't have a drain inserted and I hadn't seen the feces leaking out of my body.

I kept telling myself that I was healthy and my odds of having a successful surgery and recovery were better than most, so there was no need to even think about dying. I began to plan for my recovery, which included the time I'd need to remain in the hospital. I called my family and husband and never explained the risk to them because I didn't want to think about the possible negative outcome. I had faith that my recovery would be better than most. I assured them that there was nothing to worry about, and because of my current health condition and how quickly I was going to have the operation, the outcome was expected to be favorable, which it was.

Before the operation, I said a prayer and asked Jesus to take care of me for the next few hours, and if it was His will that it was time for me to join Him in heaven, then to please take care of my family. I asked for His forgiveness for my sins and thanked Him for taking care of me. I was at peace knowing there was nothing I could do, and the outcome was out of my hands.

There is no doubt that fear and anger was the first reaction I had, and I consciously had to change those thoughts. And as you have already concluded, I recovered from the surgery without infection, which is very surprising based on the amount of feces that had entered my body.

Imagine if I had continued to think negatively. Is it possible that my outcome could have been different? I know for a fact that I would have unnecessarily put stress on my family. The body and mind cannot be separate. But whenever a negative thought entered my mind, I replaced it with my ideas of good health. And beliefs of my faith.

I share this with you not to convince you to become Christian but to share with you the attitude I developed after realizing the outcome was out of my control, and I let go of fear and anger.

When you understand that things are out of your control, you accept that to be the case and allow things to play out with a positive, faithful attitude. By doing so, you can develop peace with the situation.

I want to address having faith. There is something to be said for believing in a positive outcome. Having faith in a favorable outcome. Faith that because there's a will, there will be a way that gives you the desired result.

Your attitude does affect your outcome.

Letting go of fear, worry, and other negative emotions allows you to focus more on the things you can control and accept those you cannot. If you're thinking about things that might never happen, you're wasting a lot of time and energy, feeling miserable for no reason. Only if you can change the outcome does it make sense to give it any attention.

Accepting uncertainty allows you to live in the moment rather than wonder about what might happen in the future. This is important because it's only when you take things as they are now that you can move on with contentment and hope.

Catching Destructive Thought Spirals

A negative thought spiral is when you think about something in a negative way that causes you to become emotional, which leads you to feel even more negatively. This cycle can happen very quickly, and it's essential to understand how it happens to avoid the negative thought spirals that might be affecting your life.

The best way to prevent this is by being aware of everything happening in your surroundings and realizing when something causes you to feel negativity. When you find yourself thinking negative thoughts, just stop. Recognize that you control your thoughts and will not allow these thoughts to ruin your mood or day. Change your thoughts to something more pleasant immediately because once the spiral begins, it will be much harder to control.

When you notice that you're thinking about something that doesn't help you and makes you feel worried, angry, or any other negative emotion, stop thinking about it and redirect your attention to something positive.

It's also a good idea to try and catch these negative thoughts before they start. For example, if you are upset about the political environment after watching a political news channel, stop watching that channel so much.

It might be a good idea to write down everything that triggers negativity, avoid those things, or reduce them in your life. You can also try using affirmations like 'I have a positive self-esteem' or 'I am confident' to bring yourself back into focus on the positive things in life.

One of the affirmations I use relates to other people's behaviors: *"I am not going to allow this person's negative attitude to affect my day. I control my attitude, not them."*

Getting rid of negative thoughts is imperative because it will do us no good if we always think negatively. These thoughts only make us feel worse and don't solve anything. We need to learn how to control them and stop thinking negatively because it won't help us achieve our goals, and it's simply less enjoyable going through life filled with negativity.

You must understand that everything in your life is not in your control. The only things you can control are your thoughts and your actions. That is where you must focus your efforts if you desire to have an enjoyable life. When you're thinking about things that are out of your control, do not allow yourself to speculate negatively. Turn it around and imagine positive outcomes.

Think of all those times when things turned out all right, even after you thought the opposite. This shows that you experienced the pain associated with negative thoughts that weren't necessary. The sooner you let go of your negative thought patterns, the more you will experience things as they are, giving you a much more enjoyable perspective on life.

Distracting the Brain

We've covered what overthinking is, how it affects your life and how you can change negative thoughts into positive thoughts. Now it's time to review ways to distract ourselves when we overthink so we can declutter our minds. Let's start with one easy thing that you can do from anywhere.

Relaxed Breathing

There's something magical about breathing. When you lose focus and are thinking about something stressful, it's a good idea to take a moment and focus on your breathing. Breathing has a very calming effect on the mind, allowing us to disconnect from what's happening around us and relax. This gives your mind some time to calm down and focus your energy on something that benefits you more than worrying about things that likely don't matter or things that are out of your control. You'll feel calmer and more relaxed as oxygen enters your body.

The first thing to do when you're stressed is to stop overthinking, direct your thoughts to a pleasant memory and focus on your breathing. This will allow your mind to calm down and help you relax, making it easier for you to take the negativity out of your thoughts and make better decisions. There's no better way of distracting your mind than breath work and focusing on pleasant memories as soon as possible.

Box breathing is an option and one of my favorites. It's not only relaxing but good for your health. During box breathing, you must keep negative thoughts away. Consider visualizing a peaceful, beautiful, happy place or positive memories.

You inhale to a count of four, hold your breath with your lungs full of air for a count of four, exhale for four, then hold your breath with empty lungs for four. Deep breathing, like box breathing, is suitable for relieving stress and anxiety and helps reduce blood pressure.

Numbers Games

Mentally demanding tasks can be a great way of losing your thoughts and directing your attention to something else. Numbers games are an option. The human brain is programmed to remember numbers; if you change your thoughts to a numbers game, your thoughts will soon be consumed.

You can start counting the stop signs you see on the way to work, how many friends and family birthdays you remember, or even how many gray cars you see on the road, etc. It doesn't matter what you're counting; count anything, and your thoughts will follow.

If you haven't played Sudoku, that is a good numbers game that takes all your focus. Check it out.

Recite Something

Try learning a poem or a few words you can recite. This will help get your mind off whatever is giving you stress and will distract it from anything that might be bothering you. It's good to know that even the most stressful situations have an upside. When we learn to cope with adversity, we gain confidence and grow as people. So, looking at the good parts of life and not focusing on the negative can do you much good.

I had what I referred to as a theme song that I would sing when I got stressed. It had happy, empowering lyrics and was upbeat, and I couldn't ever be mad or depressed when singing this song. Find a theme song that makes you happy and learn the lyrics. It's challenging to sing a happy song and have negative thoughts.

Learn Something New

This method is easy for all types of people because we can all learn new things every day in our lives, so by learning something new, we'll always be able to find a distraction if things don't go our way. Learn something 'simple' or 'easy,' like how to write your name in cursive backward or how to play a new song on the guitar, and you'll be able to focus your thoughts on something else if things get too stressful.

It's essential to be able to recognize when you're overthinking. It might take a little time before you instinctively realize that you are doing it. Still, if you keep practicing these little tricks to prevent you from overthinking and cluttering your mind, your overthinking habit will soon disappear.

Journaling

Journaling is a great way to get your thoughts or concerns to be more organized and give them structure. Journaling doesn't have to be complicated - all it requires is to write down everything on your mind calmly, and I suggest you do this with the most positive spin you can imagine.

Writing out your thoughts will allow you to notice patterns and start thinking less emotionally about what's going on in your life. It will also make it easier for you to detect patterns of things that upset you or are stressful, so that you can avoid those situations in the future.

We've experienced our minds going into overdrive when stressed, which we all know is never good. Our mind goes into overthinking mode, and we start worrying about minor things. By reminding yourself that those negative thoughts are not worth it, you'll be able to regain control of your thoughts faster than you think.

It's sometimes therapeutic to think things through, but when your thoughts move into a full-blown overthinking machine, and they start to make you feel worse than when you first started thinking about the topic, it's time to pull yourself out of this negative pattern so that your sanity is preserved, and you can move on with your day free from stress and anxiety. Remember that you can decide to be happy and stress-free. You can choose what thoughts to think about and change those thoughts at will. You can if you choose to.

Gratitude

Chapter 4

Do your thoughts shape your beliefs, or do your beliefs shape your thoughts? Either way, it's a two-way street. Both are true. From a young age, we've been conditioned to believe that what we believe influences what we think and changes how we act. Since we know that thoughts have significant power over our beliefs and that beliefs control our actions, we can see how this cycle can adversely affect our lives.

Your thoughts either support your current beliefs or challenge them. But more importantly, your thoughts can not only change your beliefs, but they are also the number one contributor to your happiness.

Gratitude changes your focus from life's difficulties to life's possibilities by opening your mind up to more opportunities and bringing them into your experience. It also allows you to expand your perspective to see a larger picture in which you are cared for and supplied with access to more abundance than you ever dreamed possible.

Most of us never really consider that how we feel and act is a direct or indirect result of our thoughts. Our thoughts are interconnected, and whether consciously or not, our thoughts influence everything in our lives. They even correlate to our health.

If you want to change your life, you must change your thoughts.

Think of a time when you were feeling happy - maybe after a great day at work or coming home to a loving partner. Perhaps you have a wonderful family that has always been there for you. What thoughts went through your mind when you were this happy?

But there were other times when it seemed that everything was going wrong, and nothing seemed to be going your way.

Between these two situations, one thing is for sure, your thoughts in the first scenario were much more pleasant than in the second. I bet you were much more enjoyable to be around the day you were happy than when nothing was going your way. Of course. That is only natural.

We can use this comparison to understand better why people, including yourself, act differently in different situations. When your thoughts are negative, you're not very enjoyable to be around. When they are positive, anyone would be happy to spend time with you.

Life is Good

I've got a new theme song. It's a song by the Zac Brown Band; Life is Good Today. The last line of the chorus says, "*Life is good today. Life is good today.*" The lyrics talk about a man moving from Georgia to somewhere in Mexico, I think, but that's not why it's my theme song. I like it because he has the most positive outlook all the time, and even when something doesn't go his way, he is grateful for the simple things in life, which makes life good today.

The gratitude expressed in this song reminds me of how grateful I am to have accomplished what I've accomplished in life. It reminds me that I have much to be thankful for no matter what happens today. If you don't have an attitude of gratitude, it is challenging to get past tough times.

The more thankful you are for everything you have and all you have experienced and have become, the happier you will be. I'm convinced that the more grateful you are, somehow you are given more opportunities to be grateful. Life has a way of working out that way. Not to mention that when we focus on the good things in our lives, we feel happier than when we focus on the difficult things. There is no doubt about that.

Setting goals and achieving them is another area in which you can express gratitude. People who focus on their most important goals are happier and more successful than those without goals.[4] By setting goals, you're more likely to achieve them,[5] and by achieving goals, you have accomplishments to be grateful for. It's a positive spiral that keeps you feeling good about your life. You make goals and achieve higher levels of success than without them, giving you something to be grateful for.

Gratitude is a central part of healing and essential to our happiness.

The more grateful you are in life, the more mentally healthy you will be. Gratitude can help with everything from medical issues to finding the right career to mental health issues. The research found that people who were grateful for their health had much lower levels of stress hormones than people who weren't focused on gratitude.[11] [6] Gratitude is critical because it makes us feel good about ourselves and gives us a sense of meaning in life.

How Being Grateful Impacts Our Life

In a study by Robert Emmons and Michael E McCullough, researchers found that grateful people were significantly happier than those who weren't grateful.[12]

Gratitude directly affected how happy or unhappy a person was. They also found that grateful people were much less likely to be depressed, anxious, or stressed. They had lower levels of stress hormones compared to those who weren't thankful and had higher levels of the happiness hormone dopamine.[7] When you are grateful, you're even more likely to make friends.[9] Gratitude also has many health benefits. Let's start with the one that will keep the doctor away.

An Improved Immune System

Oxytocin is a hormone that helps us bond with others and is also why we want to help others. When people are grateful, they secrete more oxytocin, strengthening their immune system. This happens because when we're thankful, it makes our mind focus on things other than itself and the resulting positive emotion improves the body-mind connection. Feeling gratitude enables people to reduce stress,[8] anxiety, and depression and increases resilience to cope better with all stressful situations.

It has been shown that social bonds can increase oxytocin secretion, which activates the HPA axis (hypothalamus-pituitary-adrenal axis) and boosts immune system functioning. Oxytocin also enhances glucose tolerance, a hormone linked to heart health.

Lower Blood Pressure

Isn't it interesting that we can manage lifestyle diseases like obesity, diabetes, and heart disease just by practicing gratitude? According to Robert A. Emmons, practicing gratitude can lower blood pressure. There is a correlation between feelings of gratitude and lower blood pressure, especially in people with hypertension. The reason behind this is that gratitude has a positive effect on the heart. It reduces stress, which helps lower blood pressure, and it also helps relieve symptoms of depression.

Think of the last time you appreciated someone for doing something good for you. It could have been something simple like saying 'thanks' when someone held the door for you, or it could have been a much bigger favor, such as lending you enough money to get you through the month. How did it make you feel? Did you feel good or experience a rush of incredible sensations? Gratitude can cause an upbeat sensation in your chest as if a helium balloon was inflated under your sternum. It also can cause you to feel like you want to do something nice for them, to show them how grateful you are.

Receiving a favor or kind act from someone else is often enough to make you feel good. Think of how it makes you feel when a stranger smiles at you or says 'hello' as they walk past you. You probably will smile back, feeling happy inside. The more you appreciate someone, the more willing and eager you are to express gratitude for their actions.

Gratitude Helps to Face Tough Times

When life throws you a curveball, you can't always figure out how you're supposed to react. Sometimes, your response is to feel frustrated and disappointed with yourself. Eventually, you learn that the hard times might be necessary, like a splash of cold water on your face. It can help you grow and become wiser in the process. Adversity can also be a blessing in disguise because it can give you the chance to appreciate things more deeply and face what you've been avoiding in your life.

When everything is going well, our finances are in order, our relationships are stable, and we have our health, happiness, and security, it's easier to focus on the positive things in life, like being grateful for all the things we have. However, in times of trial and tribulation, it can be hard to see everything we have as a blessing. We might feel resentful or bitter about some things in our lives. Although we don't like to admit it, sometimes our wish for things to be different can turn into a deep-seated resentment and the feeling that we don't deserve the blessings of life already present.

We'll never achieve prosperity and happiness if we're attached to the things we don't have. However, when faced with hardship and difficulty, what helps is remembering all that's good in our lives and focusing on what's positive.

Gratitude in times like this is a coping mechanism. When we learn to see the lesson in adverse circumstances, we have a firmer grasp on the things that matter in life. This is true for our relationships, career, and plans, to name just a few.

Gratitude can help us face suffering and hardship with more maturity and objectivity because it creates more distance between us and the situation. It makes it easier to see what we want instead of what we don't like and what we can do instead of what we can't do.

It's like reviewing the pictures in our photo album or the notes in our diary. We get a different perspective on them. We can see the joy we once felt and the wisdom we never noticed. Gratitude helps us see our difficulties differently and reminds us of all the good things we've forgotten or ignored.

Gratitude Opens Doors

It's no secret that we're motivated to achieve our goals by the rewards of meeting them. We want a promotion or a raise because we want more money to buy more things, pay off debt, and support our family or ourselves after retirement. But there's another source of motivation and fulfillment which might be more important than money. It's gratitude for what we already have.

Being grateful for what we have can motivate us to work harder towards our goals and lives rather than being overwhelmed by the distractions, such as money, possessions, or recognition. It gives us a better sense of purpose because it makes us realize that life is a gift. It's what we make of it that counts.

When we appreciate the things in our lives, we can focus on what motivates us to be the best version of ourselves. We can create the life we want and deserve by being grateful for all the blessings already in our lives. It makes us more of a genuine person instead of someone who pretends to be someone they're not. We begin to control our attitudes and feelings by being thankful for what is already in our lives.

Taking things for granted can create a sense of neglect in our life. We might begin to look for something, people, and experiences that will make us happier, yet we continue to be dissatisfied with the things already in our lives.

When we learn to be grateful for what we have, it's easier to see opportunities all around us. These might be opportunities to travel or work on something new, or it might be an opportunity to spend more time with family or strengthen our relationships with friends. Gratitude helps us face situations in life by realizing that there's little we need or want that can't be found right here and right now.

Ways To Practice Gratitude

Counting Blessings

Take a moment every morning and night to stop what you're doing and say 'thank you' out loud. Maybe you're grateful because you have a job, food to eat, and a roof over your head. Perhaps you're thankful because of the people in your life and the gifts they've given you. Maybe it's because of your health or the time to do what you love.

Even immaterial things, like the freedom to speak your mind and move about where you please, can be a gift that may not have been available to people in the past. And we shouldn't forget that we have time to enjoy life! Time is one of the most precious gifts we have.

If you have faith in God or another higher power, you might even want to thank God or your higher power on your gratitude list. It's always a good thing to remember that not everyone has been as blessed as you.

Maintaining a gratitude journal, or at a minimum, a list of things you're grateful for can help you track some of the blessings you've previously been given. You can jot down a few things daily or weekly if you like. Make sure you include as many items as possible, such as peace, love, and contentment. You can say them out loud, write them in a letter or even jot them down on post-it notes that you stick around the house or on your cubicle walls at work.

Tell Someone You Love Them

Who needs to hear you say, 'I love you?' Perhaps a friend loved one, or relative. You can tell them in person, on the phone, or via email or text. You can say it at the end of a day, when you're going home after work, and wish them well. When you're in the middle of something important, and your mind is focused on the task, snap out of it and tell someone you love them. This is especially good for those people who have been put on hold because it's easy to be distracted by yourself or what's missing from your life. Tell that person how much you appreciate them and remind them of all you have together.

This simple step can significantly improve estranged relationships. It's a good reminder that you've taken something for granted and that it is worthwhile to go back to the source of your connection to build a stronger bond.

That friend who had your back when you were down might need to be reminded of your appreciation. The spouse who supported you when times were tough might be feeling unappreciated. Maybe it's your parent who helped you get where you are now. Please step back and acknowledge them for what they've done for you. Your son or daughter, husband or wife, best friend, and even your pet can all benefit from it.

Take a Walk in Nature

An excellent source of gratitude is enjoying the views only nature can provide. Take a bike ride, walk, or run in your neighborhood, on nearby trails, or even around town if you have the time to do so. The scenery will amaze you, and your body will start to feel better as you get more oxygen and exercise. Some people find it relaxing to lie on the grass for an hour, look at the sky and clouds, and listen to birds or other animals around them. Remember this suggestion when we discuss being mindful, as it's appropriate to practice together.

Walking barefoot is another option that you might want to consider. I realize this might sound a little odd, but it is not only is it good for your feet, but it soothes the soul as well. You might want to soak in some sun, sit on your back patio, or hang out on a blanket in the front yard with friends.

Gratitude can't be forced, but if you look for things to appreciate while taking a walk or going about your day, you'll find it everywhere if you look for it.

You'll appreciate the butterflies for the beauty they bring to life. The trees and flowers might give you some ideas on improving your yard or garden, while the birds and squirrels will entertain you with their antics.

You'll look at the sunset as it reflects in the water and notice its beauty, which you can always appreciate no matter where you are.

You might even smile at a person walking down the street because they're wearing a fashionable shirt or perhaps a striking pair of shoes. The point is, don't forget to appreciate what is right in front of you! All of it! Take more time to enjoy everything because it's a gift that can help you be happier and healthier.

Stay Away from Negative News

Social media likes to fill our newsfeeds with news and opinions about whatever is happening in the world. Sometimes this can be bad for your mental health and spirit. It seems that the more something bothers you, the more likely it will appear in your feed. This may be annoying and unhealthy for you if you dwell on it.

If you're constantly inundated with negativity, try selecting a news feed that isn't filled with the same negative talk about politicians, celebrities, or other random pieces of most often useless information.

Follow inspirational stories about people overcoming everyday obstacles that seem impossible to overcome. The point is, don't allow the media to fill your mind with negativity and then complain about it when it begins turning you crazy.

Social media sites thrive on negativity because that's what their user base likes to read. Finding positive news and sharing it with your friends can help counteract the harmful content and make you feel less bitter about something so often portrayed in a negative light.

Be Generous

Generosity isn't just limited to giving money. It's also important to help others and let them know you're concerned about their well-being. Don't be afraid to ask people how they're doing and lend a helping hand when possible or listen to what they have to say without saying you agree or disagree with them. Letting someone know you appreciate their efforts will lift their spirits while encouraging them when they fail can help guide them towards the right path. You might not always be correct, but it's the thought that counts, and making people feel less alone can make a difference in their well-being.

Is Dave from accounting wearing a nice shirt? Be generous with your compliments. Let him know that you think he looks good today. Did your friend write a great article about a political topic? Tell them how much you enjoyed reading it and ask for more material.

It's not just about being kind to others. It's also essential to be kind to yourself. For example, if you've been eating unhealthy food all week, don't wait until tomorrow to start eating healthy. Change now, or your weight will continue to increase, or your health will continue to decline.

Gratitude and generosity are the same as they relate to how it makes us feel and are pleasant distractions to the mind. You will notice that it's tough to be unhappy when these are the thoughts that consume your mind.

Mindfulness

Chapter 5

The human mind is malleable. The things we choose to focus our minds on can significantly impact how we feel. If you spend your time thinking, 'I am fat' or 'I am clumsy,' you will feel that way and plant seeds in your subconscious mind that will grow into truths and beliefs. And these beliefs will influence your behavior and how you feel about yourself. By focusing on good things in your life, you can feel greater happiness and less stress.

Mindfulness is the art of observing our thoughts and feelings but not judging or analyzing them. We notice and then let go. It is a way to observe and accept our internal experience in the present moment non-judgmentally.

Mindfulness has been shown to reduce stress and improve overall mental health. It is so effective that many clinical studies are currently testing it in treating clinical depression[3] and anxiety.[22]

One of the main ways mindfulness benefits your mind and well-being is by reducing stress. It can help you connect to the present moment and understand how you feel, even if you are anxious or upset. When you think about something you aren't happy about, such as how your boss yelled at you for something thoughtless, or a stressful board of directors meeting that didn't go as planned, you start to feel nervous or upset about what has happened. But when you spend time with mindful awareness of your thoughts and emotions without dwelling on them or over-analyzing them, you can see that what has happened doesn't matter much in the grand scheme.

Have you ever noticed that when you are doing something like exercising, you get lost in the rhythm of it? Or when conversing with a friend, your mind wanders off to something else? We all slip into mindless states throughout our day. This is normal. But this is not mindfulness.

These mental 'spaces' give our brains opportunities to rest. Noticing this can be helpful because it reminds us that we need to relax and recharge. It also helps maintain perspective by causing us to realize that our minds will take control of our thoughts if we let them.

When mindful, we don't judge anything as right or wrong, good or bad. Our minds notice things without judgment.

Mindfulness means being aware of your surroundings, thoughts, and feelings in the present moment. Mindful awareness involves three components:

- observing the present moment

- non-judgmentally accepting and understanding of how we are feeling and what we are experiencing

- focusing on purposeful behavior rather than automatic physical reactions or habits.

Your mind can be tricky. It comes up with all sorts of things that it wants you to think or feel.

How Mindfulness Helps

Isn't it interesting that while we cannot control the unfortunate events that life throws at us, we can control how we react to them, and being mindful can help.

Mindfulness is characterized by being non-judgmental, present-oriented, and accepting. It doesn't mean we don't get angry, scared, or have negative thoughts, but it helps us deal with such situations more effectively. It helps us maintain balance and equanimity in the face of stress. The goal is to increase our awareness of positive and negative life events rather than allowing them to sweep over us and control our emotions like a raging river.

Mahatma Gandhi used the concept of the *"inner world"* and the *"outer world"* to explain the concepts underlying mindfulness. According to him, everything in life reflects what is inside us. Our outer world is simply a mirror image of our inner world.

While you cannot change the outer world for everyone around you, you can change and improve your inner world by developing mindfulness. And by changing your inner world, your outer world will change.

There are several benefits associated with being mindful, but here are some which have been specifically shown to help boost mental well-being:

Relieve Stress

An analysis of over 200 studies revealed that mindfulness-based therapy (MBT) was just as effective as cognitive behavioral therapy (CBT) for treating stress, anxiety, and depression.[14] Cortisol, a stress hormone, is released whenever we experience stress. Higher levels of cortisol in our body have been associated with high blood pressure and increased risk of cardiovascular disease. Mindfulness-based therapies help reduce cortisol levels in our bodies and lower the risk of heart disease.

When you focus on what you're feeling and experiencing in the present moment, not memories and future concerns, your body and mind produce endorphins that act as painkillers. The state of being mindful also produces dopamine, which is responsible for regulating emotions like confidence, happiness, and joy. It's referred to as the 'feel good' hormone.

We can feel less stressed and happier by paying attention to what we are feeling and experiencing in the present moment.

Curing Mild Disorders

Exercising, long walks, and even cleaning our homes can help alleviate depression and anxiety. It has also been shown that mindfulness-based therapies can significantly improve the symptoms of mild depression or anxiety. The key here is to keep moving forward, staying active, and being mindful of how we react to our moods.

Anxiety is an unpleasant emotion that arises in our mind because of fear of the future, failure, or the unknown. When we know that 'there is no cause for worry,' anxiety can be reduced significantly quickly.

Paranoia is an unhealthy fear of the intentions of others. Thinking about our neighbors and friends acts as a stressor in our minds. Mindfulness can help us overcome these negative thoughts and develop a positive outlook on life.

We start to see that anxiety and fear are born out of worry, fear, or negative beliefs about ourselves or the future. Mindfulness helps us let go of all such emotions and replace them with clarity.

Emotional Intelligence Improves

People with high levels of emotional intelligence can develop and maintain relationships, solve problems, and interact more effectively in social situations. Self-awareness is a crucial ingredient in the development of emotional intelligence.

The concept of self-awareness sounds simple, but when we realize that our thoughts help create our emotions, we start to see how important it is for our well-being.

The benefits of being mindful are not limited to improving mental health. It also helps us gain a greater awareness of who we are as individuals and increases our motivation to accomplish goals previously thought unreachable or too difficult. Mindfulness creates space for us to accept ourselves just as we are.

Our social interactions become a learning experience. We realize that life can sometimes seem unfair, and we get frustrated or angry. But in mindfulness, we can deescalate emotions and recognize these things calmly.

We start to cherish what we have, connect more to our friends and family, and become more constructive and supportive.

Interaction With Others Improves

As we become more aware of our thoughts, feelings, and those of others, it is easier for us to understand how people think. In the long run, it helps us build stronger relationships and connect with the people around us on a deeper level.

It doesn't mean that mindfulness makes life any less stressful or that there are no more challenges that we must face. Life has its ups and downs, but by improving our awareness of ourselves and our emotions, we can improve how we handle situations and control our emotions rather than allowing them to control us.

We start to see everything as a learning experience, take things less seriously and feel happier about life.

Strengthen Your Mental Core

Challenges in life often test our ability to stay positive and continue with a positive attitude. Mindfulness helps us to maintain an optimistic outlook and a more serious mind.

When you are mindful, you are less likely to act impulsively. You are aware of your needs, desires, and rights in any given situation. Eventually, being mindful also helps build confidence and awareness about your career and personal goals like relationships and health.

How to Meditate

63.6% of people reported that meditation helped them improve their concentration, boost their energy, and increase their productivity.[13] While there are no fixed rules in meditation, a certain amount of practice and focus are needed to reap the benefits.

A popular saying is, '*The more you practice, the better it gets.*' And one of my favorites is, '*Repetition is the mother of skill.*' With that said, I understand that we can't practice for long hours every day. However, I suggest you meditate for 20-30 minutes twice weekly at a minimum. Ideally, you could do this daily. If you don't have the time to do this daily, even ten minutes of meditation on alternate days will be beneficial.

How often and how long you meditate depends on your personal preference and the time you have available. Some people like to meditate twice daily, while others prefer spending less time each day in silence. You can also meditate in different ways, such as sitting or walking if that works better for you. I prefer meditating while lying in bed immediately before I start my day.

Did you know that deep breathing while sitting is quite effective in clearing the mind when cluttered, too?

When you breathe deeply, it helps calm your nervous system and makes you more physically relaxed. You also stimulate the part of your brain called the amygdala, which is responsible for stress management. The result is that you feel calmer and less anxious.

You can meditate to clear your mind whenever you feel like your brain is foggy and you can't think straight.

1. Find a calm place to sit: a peaceful place without much noise or distraction. The bedroom is an excellent place to meditate, especially if you intend to meditate at night. Make sure to silence your phone, not vibrate.

2. Sit down with a straight posture or lay flat on your back. For starters, the lotus position is not necessary, and you can sit any way that is comfortable for you. Sitting with your spine erect and your body relaxed is recommended. It's better if your back is straight and you don't slouch while sitting. If on a chair, do not tilt the back; keep it vertical. Laying on your back is also an option.

3. Close your eyes and let go of all mental clutter. This helps you focus more and give your brain a rest from the outside world. It is not necessary to close your eyes when you meditate, but it is a good idea to shut off all distractions.

4. Breathe deeply and focus on your breathing. This is the most critical step. If you have never meditated before, this is what will help you the most. When you breathe, try to be aware and focus on the breath as it travels through your nose and into your lungs. Breathe in deep for about 4 seconds before exhaling slowly for 4 - 6 seconds. Repeat this slowly for about 10-15 repetitions.

   This will help calm down your nervous system and filter out the negative thoughts in your head. You could start with four deep breaths if you feel like it is time for a break! While breathing deeply, try not to rush through it or force yourself – let each breath come naturally as you focus on getting rid of the unwanted thoughts that clutter your mind.

5. Be aware of the thoughts that come into your mind while meditating. Observe as your brain wanders and makes you think of things. The idea here is to observe each thought that comes in as it occurs but not to linger on a particular thought or follow it. When your mind wanders, let go and bring it back to the breath each time. Don't worry if thoughts keep coming up – this is

natural and sometimes happens during meditation. Although as thoughts enter your mind, release them with your exhale.

Your family, your career, random events in the past, your phone, etc. – all these things can pop up in your mind as you concentrate on your breathing. Don't be discouraged by it. Accept that it has happened and let go of the thought each time. Bring your focus back to breathing and observe as more thoughts come into your mind.

6. Stay focused on breathing, and do not stress if you get distracted. The more you practice meditation, the easier it becomes to stay distraction-free. Don't get frustrated if thoughts keep popping up; instead, try getting into a flow with them and watch them come in and out of your mind like waves on the seashore.

A Habit of Mindfulness

Holistic wellness is about keeping our body, mind, and soul healthy. Mindfulness and meditation are aspects of this health plan. It's about paying attention to our thoughts and what's going on in our lives. It's about taking a moment to be mindful of the present and what is happening around us – this helps us live life fully. Next time you feel overwhelmed with stress or anxiety, practice mindfulness and take ten to twenty minutes to meditate.

Don't just do this once and say this chick is crazy; this doesn't work! Repetition is the mother of skill. As you become more proficient, it will become more effective.

Here are a couple more ways you can incorporate mindfulness into your life.

Mindful Eating

Mindful eating is when you pay attention to the food you eat while you are eating it. It is more than just eating. It's also about being aware of your thoughts, emotions, and surroundings as you eat and experiencing the flavor of what you eat. This can help you appreciate food more and be grateful for the nourishment that your body gets from it. If your mind wanders while eating, try to refocus on the sensations of eating.

While few studies have examined the relationship between mindful eating and weight loss, one by Olson and Emery found that women with the highest levels of mindful eating were the most likely to maintain a healthy weight.[15] Weight management is an added advantage since mindful eating helps us appreciate food more.

Mindful Walking

When walking, concentrate on the steps you take and be completely aware of your surroundings. If you notice a beautiful flower along the way, see it but do not dwell on it for too long – try to keep going with your walk instead of stopping and smelling the roses! Think about it – have you ever been that grateful for your surroundings when rushing in a hurry? When walking, take as many steps as possible without thinking of anything else, and enjoy the experience of being in nature. This can help you appreciate nature more, clear the mind, and be grateful for what your body is getting from the exercise.

Immersing yourself in the present moment is not easy, but I assure you it's worth a try. Mindfulness enriches life as we take in all that is happening around us and take time to be grateful for all we have.

The same can be applied to most exercise activities– walking, rowing, elliptical, skiing, bicycling, etc. The goal is to eliminate absent-mindedness as much as possible and bring more mindfulness to these activities.

Friends and Relationships

Chapter 6

Have you noticed that the older you become, the more difficult it gets to make friends? This is because we are more selective when choosing friends when we are older and tend to make friends with others like ourselves. Look at your close friends. There's likely to be a common thread that unites you.

It may be a shared work, interest, or social background. Moreover, we tend to choose friends with the same values as us. So, it makes sense that our values and beliefs are reinforced when we spend time with friends. This is productive for our mental health because friends can encourage and support us to change ourselves and improve our lives.

However, friends can also hold you back. Growth can sometimes be lonely and require making new friends as our interests, hobbies, and values change.

I want us to look at the role friendships play in our mental health, how to find the right kind of friends, and how to maintain friendships as we grow. Let's start by looking at the psychological benefits of socializing with friends.

How Friendships Benefit our Mental Health

Belonging and Purpose

Our social circle is an integral part of our lives. It's where we feel connected to people and are not alone. Close friendships are essential for well-being. Having good friends can make us feel less lonely and more satisfied with our lives, boost our energy levels, and make us happier overall.

Social support includes having supportive interactions with others and feeling emotionally supported by the people around you. Conversely, feeling socially isolated is linked to depression, anxiety, low self-esteem, and suicidal thoughts or behaviors.

Our mental health is closely connected to the quality of our relationships with other people. Support from family, friends, and colleagues can relieve mental health symptoms such as stress, anxiety, and depression. Therefore, having supportive relationships improves your mental health and well-being.

Social Validation

One of the ways we can feel good about ourselves is by receiving positive feedback from others. Friends give us this validation because they are essential to our social circle and reflect our societal values. Close friendships help people feel good about themselves and their lives through verbal or nonverbal communication like compliments, encouragement, or support in challenging situations. This increases self-esteem, which leads to a happier life overall.

If you find yourself in a solitary job, working 80 hours a week, without much or any time for this type of interaction with others, your mental health is likely to suffer.

The value we place on ourselves is linked to our accomplishments. However, friends can also help us feel more valued. They give validation, which can be crucial in times of change. Being validated by friends makes you feel more confident and less stressed, allowing you to accept change more readily and making life more enjoyable.

Stress Management

The presence of friends can play a positive role in the recovery process after intense, stressful experiences. This is because having friends during difficult times serves as support and encouragement.

A shoulder to lean on, advice, and support are vital during stress. Friends help us by being there for us when we need them. Having friends can give us a sense of purpose during challenging times in our lives and make us feel better about ourselves.

Happiness

Having an extensive network of supportive relationships through social media may not be as helpful as having close friendships that can help you create the right kind of happiness in your life. Close friendships make deep, trusting connections, which allow you to share your emotions, thoughts, and experiences with each other. This will enable you to become the best version of yourself and be happier overall.

In times of need, having friends who can tangibly help you can make all the difference in your life. Friends give support, advice, empathy, and compassion when you're going through difficult times. True good friends are there for you – unconditionally.

Coping with Trauma

Being diagnosed with a chronic illness, losing a loved one, being fired from work, or struggling with mental health problems are just a few of the many traumatic events that can happen in one's life. Friends are crucial in helping us cope with trauma because they offer helpful advice, share their experiences with similar situations, give us a shoulder to lean on, and lift us when we are down. They can make us feel less alone and more accepted for who we are.

Friends are also important when it comes to the recovery process after a traumatic event occurs. Having friends can make you feel less lonely and isolated, boost your energy levels, and make you happier overall. The presence of friends can play a positive role in your recovery after intense, stressful experiences.

When you know that you're not alone in your hardships, you can get through things more quickly and with less pain. Even if a friend is not directly affected by a traumatic event, being there for you can help immensely. Friends offer comfort and assurance that everything will be okay, and they make you feel wanted and appreciated in life.

Talking to Friends About Mental Health?

Opening up to friends about your mental health issues can be difficult and sometimes even scary. There is, however, much value in having someone close to share your experiences with.

Society has stigmatized having mental health problems, and men are more affected by this. 40% Of men have never talked to anyone about their mental health problems and would instead 'bottle it up.' They're either embarrassed, afraid of being judged, or feel too vulnerable to talk about it.[16]

Men are three to four times more likely to commit suicide than women.[17] Be open and honest if you plan to talk to your friend about your feelings and struggles. It's good to tell a friend how you're feeling, but your friend must be sensitive and listen when you talk about the difficulties you've been through.

Here's How You Can Go About It

Start by introducing the topic. 'I've been struggling with some issues lately. I was wondering if I could talk to you about it.'

Be open and honest about your experiences. Don't judge yourself because that can make things worse. Your friend must understand what you're going through, so it's best to explain why you feel the way you do or how the situation made you feel: 'I've been feeling... (sad/lost/angry/frustrated) because....'

Seek support from friends when you need it. Tell them when they can help, what they can do, and how they can help: 'Do you have time this weekend? We could go for lunch and a chat?'

Acknowledge what they say because you don't want them to feel ignored or patronized

Be open about your feelings and be sure to let them know how they make you feel. If you're having trouble discussing your feelings with a friend, try writing down your thoughts and then discussing them face to face. You can even give them what you wrote in advance, so they have time to think about it and be better able to support you.

Let people know when they can assist you in times of need. Don't be afraid to ask for help. Asking for help is not a weakness – it's a sign that you're strong, and strong people are valued by society and will be valued by a true friend.

This won't be a pity party where your friends will embarrass you. You're allowed to feel sad, frustrated, or angry and express that without feeling ashamed and true friends understand this.

I sometimes get 'peopled out.' Meeting with friends during one of these times may not be wise, so it's okay to say no to people too. If the thought of socializing makes you feel drained and stressed, it's okay if you pass and connect later. Don't allow your friendships to be a burden. Choose the right time to talk.

Surround Yourself with People that Make You Feel Good

An exciting way of taking care of our mental health is by surrounding ourselves with people who make us feel good, people we would like to be like, and at a minimum, people who lift us. I'm not talking about finding more financially successful people who've climbed the corporate ladder. Those people you can connect with for other reasons, but that's not what you're looking for when it comes to true friends.

True friends care about you, make you feel good about yourself, and are genuinely interested in your well-being, and when you're with them, you never feel anything other than their genuine feelings for you. These are the friends that can make a difference in our lives.

When you surround yourself with people who reduce your stress levels, your world becomes a better place in many ways. You become happier and feel more connected to other people, including your friends. You feel cared about and worthy.

When you have mental health struggles, you must feel accepted – but not just then, all the time. It's also important to encourage each other whether or not you're going through hard times. Friends never want to make each other feel alone and as if they have no one to talk to.

Additionally, good friends are the ones who challenge us intellectually, emotionally, and socially.

If a friend challenges you to do better, it's probably safe to say that this friendship is worth keeping. A friend who challenges you is someone who looks at you, then looks at the world and says, 'You can be better than this. We can be better than this. And together, we're going to try.' That's what it means to be challenged. And that's another reason why good friends are worth having in our lives. It's not always easy having solid opinions or being told that your views might be off base – but when a true friend shares this with you, you must know that it's something you likely need to hear.

One last note about good true friends, you must be there for them too, and remember, no pity parties. You support each other. You're never to become a burden to each other, lift each other when needed, and never get together for a gripe session. There's no good in that.

Friends and family are there for you in times of need, but mental peace and happiness don't just happen because of them. It's a process that involves work. Conscious work.

But it's not something that you have to do alone. Perspective is everything – believe in yourself, believe in good friends, and know that your life is more meaningful when you have mental peace.

Destructive Relationships

We all have that annoying neighbor or co-worker who is a negative Nelly and never stops complaining. Unfortunately, some of us have family members this way too. The problem with negative people is that they drain your energy and make you think negatively about everything around you if you let them.

Don't Give Them Your Energy

They may believe they are a good influence on you and others – but they're reducing the quality of their lives by being too hostile toward everything.

Ignore them when possible. Negativity is contagious. We tend to become negative when we listen to negative people and start believing in their pessimistic mindset. Before you know it, you're complaining about things yourself.

If you can, get away from them as soon as possible. Their negativity is not your problem. They'll drag you down if you try to change their opinion or argue with them. Not only will they remain unhappy, but they will also try to make you feel the same way.

Be optimistic yourself, and if you must work with negative Nelly, or if she's family, change the topic to something enjoyable and don't give their complaining or negative energy any more vigor to grow.

Be Assertive

The best way to deal with negative Nelly is to be firm. Just tell her, 'Hey, Nelly, I don't want to hear that story again; there's no benefit in focusing on that negativity.' This shows them that you don't want to be around them when they're complaining, and often, they will find others who partake in their hostile, useless complaining as they learn you won't allow them to be that way with you. It's not just a subtle hint or anything like that that I'm suggesting. Just level with them.

I am not saying you should tell them they are harmful or negative. I am offering you to let them know that you don't want to partake in complaining about things you cannot change. Being assertive with negative people can be challenging, however. You may need to work on your assertiveness skills. Remember not to attack the person, just the complaining at hand.

Time for a Change

If all else fails, find healthier relationships with people who look for a reason to enjoy life and be happy instead of reasons to be negative and complain. You're going to find yourself much more comfortable when you do this. Remember that you deserve positive and healthy relationships, not negative ones that will make you feel like crap about everything around you.

I realize you can't change your family or your boss (well, maybe you can), so this doesn't work in every situation, but in those that it does, there is no reason to allow their negative attitude to ruin your mood and sometimes your day. Do what works best for you but try not to associate with negative people too much, as it will have long-term effects.

In situations where you cannot get away from negative people, such as family or co-workers, you can be assertive, keep things positive, not give their negativity energy, or practice mindfulness.

Your stress levels will decrease significantly once you practice mindfulness daily and get the negative Nelly out of your life. Mindfulness will allow you to better tolerate all the negativity around you as you understand it has nothing to do with your world.

Meeting Inspiring People

The final piece of advice I'd like to give you regarding relationships is to meet inspiring and productive people. Getting to know people takes work, dedication, and patience. It also takes time. This art of getting to know people on a deeper level is more than mere socializing. It takes time and effort, but it's something that you can learn with dedicated practice if you're willing to put in the effort yourself.

I'm going to share some tips on how you can make valuable connections with others – whether at your workplace, school, or social circle.

Commonality

Hobbies, sports, interests, values, and goals build a strong foundation for any relationship. Start by finding people who share the same passions as you and try to spend time with them. You can find them at your workplace or in your daily life. With so many ways to connect with others, such as Meet Up (https://www.meetup.com), you can find others more easily with something in common.

Don't be afraid of being yourself. When developing new friendships, be who you are, not who you think you should be. But of course, don't just jump into talking about mental health if you're participating in a pickleball group. Seek out those that have positive attitudes and play more pickleball first. Develop a friendship with those that you know will ultimately be a healthy relationship for you.

Eventually, you can open up and share your own experiences. This is how you can get a deeper connection and can help each other grow. This gets easier the more you practice it regularly with different people. Start by opening up to one friend at a time – all it takes is for you to take that first step, then everything else will fall into place once you do so.

You can join a gym, book club, or yoga class to meet people who share your passions and develop new healthy friendships.

Be Genuinely Interested

Be fully present when you are talking to someone. People love it when you are interested in what they say, and they will want to get to know you better. Do not be distracted by your phone, what's happening around you, or anything else while talking with them. Connect with them and be there fully. Invest your full attention in what they are saying and be open. You will find that people will appreciate that you've taken the time out of your day to connect with them on the deepest level possible, and you'll develop meaningful relationships that way.

I realize I have suggested finding commonality with others, but remember, it is not about how much you have in common with someone else when it comes to developing meaningful relationships, but it's more about how you manage your differences; that is where unique growth opportunities occur, and deep relationships can develop.

Active listening is a beautiful way to show someone you're interested in what they say and that you see value in them.

Appreciate Their Personality

When meeting someone for the first time, look for signs of personality and be curious about their responses. For example, a person who seems confident is less likely to feel uncomfortable with compliments – so feel free to extend a genuine compliment.

If they are showing signs of being introverted, make them feel comfortable talking about themselves by asking questions to clarify what they share with you. The more comfortable they feel with you, the more they will share things they usually don't share with others.

People like people like themselves, so discussing things you have in common first helps build rapport and develop deeper relationships. If you show a genuine interest and are kind, eventually, they will start telling you more about themselves and ask more about you too. This is the beginning of what may become a long-lasting friendship.

Comfort Zone

Chapter 7

Quick question: What do business coaches and motivational speakers have in common? They love talking about 'breaking' out of our comfort zone. To them, comfort zones are prisons that keep us from reaching our true potential.

While some comfort zones are safe and nurturing, most are self-imposed limitations. If you feel bored, stuck, or unhappy with your life, you might be so locked into your comfort zone that it's stopping you from breaking free.

Breaking out of your comfort zone takes an act of will and a little bit of courage. It means you will not be comfortable; some find that a little scary. A mentor of mind says, *'there is growth in chaos.'* Chaos does not seem incredibly fun, does it? But when the chaos comes with no fear, it is enjoyable. The anticipation of something new, an opportunity to gain experience exists, and this is where good anxiety, in the form of anticipation, helps us grow.

All discomfort is not bad for our mental health. It's time to learn how to manage discomfort where we are happy, creative, healthy, fulfilled, and productive. Getting out of our comfort zone breaks down what are called 'trials' and 'traps,' ways many of us stay stuck, and offers the skills necessary to move freely in our life.

Our comfort zone refers to the boundaries we define for ourselves. Imagine that your mental and physical health are things you can wear, like clothes. When your clothes are dirty or torn, they must be washed and repaired. And this is what we do with our clothes: when they're damaged, it's time to take them to an alterations shop and get them fixed. Sometimes they're too damaged to keep, so we throw them away. If they're old or outdated, then it's time to buy new clothes. So too with our physical and mental health: if they're in bad shape, then it's time for a repair job; if necessary, even a full-on replacement.

When we're in touch with our feelings and thinking clearly and rationally, we have what is called 'mental clarity.' When we are in a mental fog and unable to think clearly, our mind will take us down a short path to a place called our comfort zone.

Self-Imposed Limitations

What do our self-imposed limitations, our comfort zone, have to do with our mental health? Our mental and physical health are products of our physical, social, and psychological well-being. Our emotional health comes from the strength of our self-esteem and our ability to think with a constructive uncluttered mind.

While our comfort zones are necessary, they can keep us from experiencing what we are truly capable of. When we are stuck in a comfort zone, we'll do everything we can to avoid moving out.

Here are the five most significant reasons why most stay trapped in our comfort zones:

Fear of Failure

We get stuck in our comfort zones because it's terrifying to think about what will happen and result from this change when we step outside them. We cling to the security of the familiar because it gives us a sense that life has some known meaning or purpose. It removes loneliness or insecurity associated with moving out of familiar surroundings and into unknown territory.

The fear of being judged for failing can often be so frustrating that we never even try. We believe that setting and reaching new goals are out of reach because we're not smart or good enough. Fear of disappointment can make us feel like we will die if we fail. But the truth is that failure is nothing more than feedback. It reveals to us what doesn't work so that we know where to focus our energy next time.

When we fail at something, we can't take ourselves too seriously. There is a silly saying I picked up along the way that

I believe originally came from a Three Stooges skit back in 1936, but it is still relevant.

If at first you don't succeed, keep on sucking until you do succeed!

I know it's a little silly. But everything we have ever done in life was hard before it became easy. I know I sucked at snowboarding the first few days I was learning. But today, I'm pretty good at it. We are not expected to be perfect, especially when trying something new.

Fear of Uncertainty

Are you willing to take a risk and try on something new, not knowing what the result will be or even how it will make you feel?

Some things are too scary to even think about because of what could happen if we fail. For example, skydiving, base jumping, scuba diving for some, etc. With these examples, there's a possibility of death. But what about these scenarios:

- Moving to a new city and starting a new job, school, or business.

- Taking a new hobby or interest, like learning the guitar, dancing, playing pickleball, or trying out for the school softball team.
- Starting a relationship with someone you barely know.
- Moving into uncharted territory: trying something that seems risky, like dating someone different from you instead of some of the people you feel comfortable with.

We build mental walls around our comfort zones to keep these changes from happening. But what's more is that once we've built walls to protect ourselves, it's difficult to tear them down again.

But these things people do all the time. It's how they find happiness sometimes. It's how they get to experience more of life. It makes their life more worthwhile. And it can be for you too.

Illusion of Comfort

Uncomfortable situations can be viewed as threats – and the fear of them can make us so anxious that we avoid getting out of our comfort zones for good, especially when things have been going smoothly.

The illusion of comfort refers to our perceptions of how we think things are going or how they should be. This illusion of comfort may not even be healthy for us, but because change is difficult, we stay stuck. We accept what isn't what we ever wanted, but it is the known, and we know we can exist there, so we stay stuck there.

Sometimes our comfort zone isn't comfortable. We are stuck in a situation where we cannot be ourselves. We have to watch every word we say and every move we make. We don't want to be perceived as a fool by saying something inappropriate or embarrassing ourselves by making mistakes. Perhaps we try so hard to please others that it becomes difficult for us to speak up for ourselves when we need to. Some people will search for silence when this happens because it's easier to hide in their comfort zones than face these fears head-on. Silence seems calmer, but it is not as healthy.

Illusion of Imbalance

Many people would rather play it safe and avoid taking risks and making mistakes. When we feel like we're not meeting our expectations or things are not going well, this can make us anxious and even numb us to negative feedback. We can't handle the uncomfortable emotions that come with the truth because they challenge our balance: how confident or secure are we feeling in ourselves? This can be a tricky question because it asks so much of us.

We revert to our comfort zones when uncomfortable things happen. But it's not because we think the world will end if we make a mistake or the sky is going to fall if someone doesn't like our work. It's because we're so used to living in our comfort zone that anything that goes wrong feels like a threat to our well-being and security. Our feelings of safety are based partly on what we expect others to think of us and how certain we are about our self-worth.

Fear of Change

Are we making real changes if we always live within our comfort zone? Our fear of change is a fear of letting go of the things that we know and love, like our family and friends. We might be afraid that if we move out on our own or try new things, we'll be worse off than if we did nothing.

We try to hold onto the security blanket so tightly that it makes us forget how strong we are. We forget how amazing and powerful the human spirit can be when it flourishes. There's this idea that you can't grow as a human unless you do something dramatic and risky. This seems like a lot of pressure and work. But what if that's not true? What if you don't have to do anything remarkable at all?

The fear of change has little to no benefit in our lives. Most changes we implement make our lives more fulfilled. We can't grow if we're stuck in our comfort zone, but a word of caution, we also can't grow if we're always moving on and changing things. The truth is that there's a balance that's needed.

Doing Challenging Things

Doing challenging things is sure to improve your self-esteem and boost your confidence. When Morgan Freeman said that, "... challenging ourselves is the only path that leads to growth," he wasn't kidding.

Challenging ourselves is something most of us avoid because it's scary as heck. But it has much more benefits than we could ever imagine. Let's take a look at why challenging yourself can be good for you:

It Improves Self-esteem

When we do challenging things, it can help us build our self-esteem and assertiveness by showing us what we're capable of when we put our minds to something and how awesome we can feel when we try something new and accomplish it. Our mental image tends to scale with the challenges we have taken up, so we must take up some.

As we conquer one challenge, the next one will become more accessible and less scary. The more we do things, the better our confidence and the more we overcome our fears.

Tom Hopkins, a sales trainer I studied when I was much younger, said something like this about fear:

"When you do what you fear most,
you control your fear."
~Tom Hopkins

It lets us push ourselves to perform at our very best. Most people avoid challenging new situations because they fear the unknown or they fear they won't handle them well. When learning something new, they even fear their results will not be good. So, some people avoid anything they are uncomfortable with. But these outcomes are rarely the case; taking up challenging things can help us improve on many other things.

Our self-esteem and mental health improve when we take up challenges. It takes your mind to a place where it will have to call upon aspects of your mentality to overcome what's in front of you, and when you do, you feel great.

For example, you decide to take a lesson in snowboarding. You fall a lot and are on your butt much of the morning, but by the end of the day, you're making it down the mountain. You had courage; you overcame your fear; you showed resolve; you had to tap into a part of your mind that only supported your self-esteem and mental health.

Building Character

Sounds corny? Perhaps. But challenging ourselves is a great way to learn and grow as individuals, and it also helps us get rid of fears and insecurities by encouraging us to overcome them. I've said it before, and I'll repeat it, we can't take ourselves that seriously, and we certainly can't be afraid to fail. We aren't expected to be perfect when trying new things. We just brush it off and move on if it doesn't work out. Even laugh at ourselves at times.

However, accomplishing something you thought you couldn't gives you the perspective necessary to face other difficulties with much more courage and confidence in the future. Courage, confidence, or an ability to deal with fear are things you can learn and build as you do more things out of your comfort zone.

Every successive challenge we overcome teaches us new things and builds our character, and the more challenges we do, the stronger and more confident we become. It helps us gain more knowledge through trial and error and teaches us to deal with failure constructively in a way that will boost our mental health.

Challenging ourselves provides us with opportunities to build character, humility, and people skills. We might suck when we start doing something for the first time, but eventually, we might also succeed. Keep on sucking until you succeed! And as we learn about ourselves by challenging ourselves, it will improve our outlook on many things, leading to a much more fulfilling life.

Discover Something About Yourself

I'm sure you can agree that most fears we deal with in our lives are irrational fears. Is there any real risk in applying to a job post and never getting invited to an interview? Or asking someone out on a date and having them not accept? No, not really. But our brain interprets these things as scary because when we've encountered things like these, we may have failed.

Challenging yourself lets you do away with this thinking because you become aware that your past failures don't predict how you will perform in the future. The more you take up challenges and overcome them, the less fearful you become. It helps you keep negative self-talk at bay and replace it with self-encouragement, which most of us rarely do enough.

You'll learn that you're not made of glass that will shatter when you're pushed just enough, and instead of beating yourself up for not being brave enough to do it, you will feel inspired to get out there and try again.

Get Out of Your Comfort Zone

The growth zone lies outside of your comfort zone. When you allow yourself to live within your self-imposed limitations and not challenge yourself, you stagnate and fall into failure. Instead, when you push your boundaries further, you grow in specific ways that make you more well-rounded and improve your understanding of others' perspectives. But it's not just our mental health that suffers when we don't do things that challenge us. Our lives tend to become stagnant, unproductive, and uninteresting.

Challenging ourselves is a crucial way to build our self-esteem and confidence by learning that we can overcome almost anything when we put our minds to it; it helps us discover more about ourselves and develop our character.

By putting yourself in healthy situations that make you uncomfortable, you force yourself to do things you're not used to, which will help you break past your initial fears. As you push yourself into these uncomfortable situations more often, your fear of them will grow less and less, you will grow stronger, and you'll discover something about yourself in the process. The stronger you become by doing what you fear and overcoming your fear leads to other positive impacts in your life.

You will become more confident and assertive. You will be more effective at controlling negative thoughts. You will know that you can accomplish what you put your mind to.

Let's say that you want to ask someone out on a date, assuming you're single, and this is out of character for you due to the fear of being rejected. Getting a 'no' is not something we want to subject ourselves to. But what if you knew that regardless of whether you got a 'yes' or 'no,' you would be given $500? Would you then take a chance? Would getting a 'no' be worth $500? If it's not worth it, then would it be worth $5,000? There's likely a number for everyone that would make this fear of rejection minuscule in the scope of what you would be rewarded.

My point is that what you gain is worth much to your character and, in the long run, your self-esteem. Overcoming your fear of rejection will add so much to your life that it would be worth more than $500, or whatever amount, to attain it. Once you care more about your perception of yourself than others' perception of you, much stress and anxiety is relieved from your life.

Consider reframing your thoughts to understand the benefit to your mental well-being when you get a sense of fear entering your mind, and soon you'll be trying to get a date with everyone... Just kidding... But I hope you see the point.

How do you tackle fear in the future? Talk through these steps with yourself.

- What are the chances of what I fear happening? If not so much, then consider how much time you are wasting with thoughts of fear and how much stress that's giving you. Reframe your thinking to the chances that this will work out the way you like instead.
- What is the best that can happen? That is where you must begin thinking. If everything goes how you want it to, what will that outcome be?
- What is the worst that can happen? Can you live with that? If so, you must give it a try.
- What can we do to minimize this outcome? If you get rejected by the man you ask out for a date, whoever will know about it other than you and him. Maybe his friends but not likely anyone you know will even know it happened, for example.
- If you can handle the worst-case scenario, and you're excited about the best-case scenario, chances are, you'll land somewhere in the middle, if not your best-case scenario, and that's nothing to be afraid of.

If you can do these things and face your fears, they will begin to drift away as if they were never there. You must challenge yourself by asking good questions when faced with the fear of rejection or failure - this is a positive way to discover what's behind your fears, and once it becomes clear that your fear is not rational, it makes you more confident and less fearful. It will also help you overcome fear faster in the future. So don't be afraid to try something new or to get out of your comfort zone. Remember, if you do what you fear most, you will conquer your fear.

Perspective

Chapter 8

Many factors in our lives impact our mental well-being, such as work and career, friendships, family life, lifestyle, and finances. All these areas can significantly impact how we feel about ourselves, how we interact with the world, and how mentally healthy we are. The things that affect us in these areas are often pushed down our priority list, which can lead to some of us not being as happy as we could be.

We must start looking at our approach towards mental health, with all aspects involved. I believe that having a holistic approach toward mental well-being means looking at all the different areas that affect your happiness and taking care of them in one big swoop. Otherwise, the importance of each aspect can be pushed down on your priority list, creating a big hole in your well-being.

A study of over 4,500 people showed that those with a growth mindset, a belief that their abilities could be cultivated, and a positive style of thought experienced more success, satisfaction, and well-being than those with a fixed mindset or negative thought patterns.[18]

Isn't it amazing that your future success can be predicted, to some degree, by how you think? The subconscious mind is constantly making decisions about whether or not you will succeed. It's essential to play to your strengths, improve your weaknesses and focus on the positive so that you are playing from a position of power.

Mental health is as much about how you think as it is about what you do mentally. Feeling good mentally may not always translate into feeling good with your physical body, but it certainly means that your mind and body align with one another. You have control over your mental health – every day, you can choose how you will feel, regardless of external circumstances. This means you can decide which thoughts, feelings, and emotions you want to be around and which behaviors will contribute to those feelings.

Positive Thinking

Our mental health directly affects our physical health. Science has shown that negative emotions can cause physiological changes, such as increased stress hormones, the activation of the fight-or-flight response, and a weakened immune system.[23] When we feel stressed or worried, we're more likely to get ill due to the chemical changes these negative emotions create in our bodies. Chronic stress has been linked with many health issues, including heart disease, the number one killer globally.

Below are some benefits of having an optimistic attitude and freeing your negativity.

Optimism Leads to Happiness

This is one of the most well-known benefits, as it's something that the media often discusses. The belief that life is good or that we're going to get what we want can lead to feelings of happiness. There's scientific evidence that optimism leads to a real, long-term boost in joy and optimistic people generally have happier lives. That seems like common sense, doesn't it?

When our mental health is positive, stress doesn't exist, or at least not for long. It's all about how our brain perceives things; when we believe something is stressful, our brain causes stress hormones to be released. I like to reframe things. When I was stressed because I had more work to complete in a week than waking hours, instead of referring to it as being stressed, I would tell myself that I was busy and I was doing as much as I could, and that was going to have to be good enough. I would say to myself that I'm more efficient than others, and they were lucky to have me because others would be accomplishing even less. So I would manage my stress by reframing it as being busy and on my productivity. And I genuinely believed everything I said above, so I could sleep at night without stress despite being busy.

In other words, stress is only as stressful as you decide. This means that a positive perspective on mental health can help us reframe stressful situations so they don't affect us significantly.

A Sense of Purpose is Liberating

A desire to achieve certain things in life can create a sense of purpose. This sense of purpose allows us to live for something more than our daily activities and have confidence that we're doing something important. When we view our lives as having meaning, it's easier to cope with the challenges, stress, and setbacks present because we believe there's a reason for them. Each person's sense of meaning is unique, based on their values and beliefs. For example, I'm passionate about holistic wellness. Therefore, my sense of purpose relates directly to my values around promoting holistic wellness.

Your self-perception can affect your self-worth: a positive self-image allows you to believe you can achieve things and be successful. When you have self-worth, you feel good about yourself, which makes you more confident and able to deal with stressful situations.

Viewing Things in a Different Light

Let's start with placing yourself in someone else's shoes who's just won the lottery. This person has just become a billionaire. What type of person do you think they are?

What do they eat? What do they wear? How do they act? What are their views on life, society, and everything else? What do you think they will buy first – a yacht, an apartment in Paris, or an island? Perhaps a sexy little sports car might also be on their shopping list – maybe even two or three of them!

The Hedonic Treadmill is an interesting psychological phenomenon. It was noted that even after a life-changing event, like winning the lottery and becoming a billionaire, people return to their 'usual' level of well-being before the event.

Many people who win the lottery blow the money and end up living not much different than they did before. And others get all of those material things we listed above and still are no happier than they were before gaining all of those things. Perhaps it's time to find happiness another way. Maybe it's time to view things in a different light.

Can you change how you think? Can you change your perception of the world? Can you learn to see differently? You will improve your life and enjoy life more fully if you can.

The good news is that our minds are essentially plastic. Neuroplasticity, the ability of our brains to make new connections, is remarkable. We can reshape our minds in many ways, for better or worse. The bad news is that even though our brains contain a seemingly infinite number of connections, our minds quickly forget and slip into our old comfort zone if we let it.

Instead, let's use these connections as tools to improve and enhance the quality of our lives.

Instead of being content with what you have (which I would recommend as a not-so-bad idea to start), why not try something new? Why not generate more happiness by seeking out some previously unknown opportunities? If you have an unusual idea that could make you more money, recognition, or love, why not pursue it now?

What about new experiences?

Manifestation

Chapter 9

In chapter 5, we learned that mindful meditation could be an effective tool to combat mental, emotional, and physical challenges. One of the critical concepts in meditation is awareness or mindfulness. Exciting things happen when we practice meditation and learn to be aware of our surroundings and mental state.

We start to get 'itchy feet.' We begin to realize that we can't stay in the same place forever. We recognize there is more than just a comfortable, cushioned life. Something drives us towards this realization, and we naturally feel compelled to leave our comfort zone, enter new territories and experience new things. We start to notice that the universe is much larger than the little world we have built for ourselves. We start to feel an urge to travel abroad, and we begin to wonder if there is more out there than what's in our heads.

This is one of the most beautiful things that can happen in meditation. It's a seed of curiosity, a sense of wonder, a yearning to know what is beyond our perception. And it is also one of the most powerful things that can happen in meditation. Because once this seed sprouts, it begins to develop its own needs and wants. The journey becomes an end in itself.

What is Manifestation

Manifestation refers to the form that an idea takes. How do we get from a concept to an actual thing in the world? The answer is with action.

Most of us manifest accidentally. We allow our thoughts to plant a seed in our subconscious mind, and manifestation is when we take action to enable the seed to become a plant. Put another way; most don't manifest things intentionally. They manifest things because they're intensely thinking about and focusing on something they don't realize can manifest with action. Therefore, it is so important to learn to be aware of our needs and desires in the first place. It's also why it is so important to be patient and kind to yourself during the process. The universe, or your higher power, helps you when you show respect for its power.

For example, if you regularly complain about your job and wish you had something different, this ultimately plays out in your performance. You might even get fired. Or you begin to search the want ads for alternate employment. But if you weren't always thinking about having a different job, those actions would not have occurred.

Another example is if you play a sport and regularly tell yourself that you'll never be any good at it, you convince yourself that is the case and don't work on the things that would help you improve.

The Law of Attraction does not explain everything, but it explains much about the nature of reality. We are naturally drawn to things we give emotional attention to as if our DNA were magnetized, so every way we go brings us closer to particular circumstances. Our subconscious mind is very attuned to figuring out ways of making things happen, even if we don't consciously realize we're doing it.

Meditation is a tool that allows you to quiet your mind and cultivate your inner world. And since your outer world is merely a reflection of your inner world, your outer world will begin to change. When you realize what manifestation means, it can feel like the universe, and your outer world is conspiring against you.

When you first begin meditating, you may notice that your thoughts are somewhat chaotic, like a mob of angry trolls. You have so many ideas competing for your attention and trying to teach you why what you're doing currently is not working out.

It can be a difficult transition from focusing on one thought at a time, learning to observe every thought as just a thought, and then trying to let them go.

Physical Manifestations Caused by Mental Health

The mind-body connection is an essential aspect of your mental health. Physical symptoms may result from mental states or are triggered by their presence. For example, depression affects the body's functions and can cause physical symptoms such as fatigue, headache, and weight loss. Therefore, recognizing and evaluating the physical manifestations of mental health issues is essential to successfully treating them.

Here we'll be looking at ways mental health concerns present themselves physically. There are various physical manifestations of mental health issues. The mind and body cannot operate separately. When there's distress in the mind, it will show in the body automatically. Our subconscious minds have tremendous power. Sometimes it can work to our benefit, but sometimes it does not.

Change in Sleeping Patterns

Our sleeping habits are affected by several factors, including our mental well-being. An increase or decrease in sleep can be caused by emotions such as worry, fear, or anger. For example, someone who has just argued with their partner might find they cannot sleep that night. This could indicate emotional distress.

When we're stressed, for example, we may have trouble sleeping. Stress is a common cause of insomnia, as the increased cortisol makes it difficult to stay asleep. Stress can lead to fatigue and can also be responsible for causing us to sleep too much.

A lack of motivation or concentration can be associated with anxiety and depression. Someone suffering from a mental health disorder, stress, or anxiety may have difficulty staying awake at work or school.

Feeling drowsy and lack of interest in the world around you could result from depression, especially if it accompanies other symptoms such as a change in appetite, low mood, and thoughts about suicide.

Change in Eating Habits

Our eating habits include how often we eat, how much we eat, and how food is prepared. A change in eating habits could indicate a mood or mental health change. A lack of appetite could be a symptom of depression. If the person's weight is affected, this is another indication of depression.

However, many changes in eating patterns do not necessarily indicate mental health issues. They could be due to unrelated lifestyle changes such as gaining or losing weight, starting or stopping exercise, etc.

Change in Lifestyle

Skipping the gym, failing to meet deadlines at work, reduced interest in grooming and personal hygiene... These are some signs of mental illness and sometimes are easy to miss.

These tell-tale warning signs can be the first indication that someone suffers from a mental health issue – anxiety, depression, bipolar disorder, or schizophrenia.

While many people will shrug these warning signs off, you should know that these are also some of the most common symptoms shown by those developing a severe mental illness.

What starts as a disinterest in personal hygiene can quickly become a complete aversion to keeping clean. The same is true of social or cultural events. For example, someone with schizophrenia may begin to hate all sounds coming from other people's mouths or become obsessed with the sound of their voices.

Social Withdrawal

Social behaviors are one of the first things to be affected by mental health disorders. In the early stages, this can take the form of something as simple as not returning phone calls from friends or family members. Social withdrawal can turn into a complete fear of leaving the house, and when this happens, it can develop into agoraphobia.

If you notice that your loved one is withdrawing from their circle of friends and family, but they don't seem to have any specific reason for doing so, it could be a sign that something deeper is going on.

Aggressive and Hostile Behavior

It's natural to feel angry or frustrated sometimes – everyone does – but when those feelings become uncontrollable and are directed at the people closest to you, it may be time for concern. A simple test in this area worth trying is to bring up a subject that usually provokes an emotional response.

Excessive anger is a common symptom of depression, bipolar disorder, and schizophrenia and can happen without warning. It can be hard to tell if someone is genuinely angry or depressed.

One of the best ways to determine if someone has anger issues is to witness their reaction towards others who don't deserve their negative feelings. Dramatic mood swings, as well as constant feelings of jealousy, are other tell-tale signs.

Delusions

Hallucinations, delusions, and paranoia may seem like signs of mental illness to outsiders, but they're just as much part of the disorder's realm. Delusions are also known as false beliefs. People with schizophrenia say things like, 'I'm being followed by a spy' or 'The CIA is after me' when no one sneaks around behind them.

Other delusion forms include the belief that their loved ones are trying to have them committed or have taken away their children. Or the idea that something sinister is happening in their home and being broadcast over television.

In extreme cases, someone suffering from delusions may find themselves 'hiding' in their bedroom for hours, convinced that people are trying to harm them.

Inability to Concentrate on Tasks

Our cognitive abilities are the things that help us think, learn and process information. When stressed, we experience brain fog – a lack of concentration and an inability to process information. The symptoms of mental illness are almost always accompanied by slower thought processes, which can interrupt daily activities – at work, home, or school.

Anxiety, for example, produces brain fog in the form of 'mental rambling' – a constant stream of irrelevant, negative thoughts. As a result, we can't concentrate and become distracted by our thoughts instead.

When we experience brain fog, it's incredibly frustrating because it feels like something is wrong with us. There are many reasons this is a common side effect of anxiety. Cognitive impairment is so common among those with mental disorders and illnesses.

Feelings of Helplessness

This is a behavior rather than a symptom, but the two are often intermingled. For example, someone who becomes suicidal may say, 'My life is meaningless,' or 'What's the point?' These statements sound like thoughts and feelings to anyone, but for someone who suffers from severe depression or bipolar disorder, these are just as real as suicide, as a possible response to their mood.

Physical Pain

Can you believe that anxiety has been proven to increase pain levels? Yes, pain is a manifestation that may seem surprising but makes perfect sense. If hormones are excreted when you're feeling good, which makes you feel even better, then they are not in abundance when you have anxiety. For example, if you have high anxiety before surgery, your postoperative pain and reliance on painkillers after surgery will be higher.[1] Imagine having high anxiety and then having an accident of some sort. You've just increased your pain.

Manifestation in Your Favor

You can see that mental health has a direct reflection on physical health. The law of attraction causes the manifestation of desires even when they are unconscious thoughts. As a functional nutrition and lifestyle practitioner, I've seen this play out in undesirable manifestations. There are definite changes to the body when your thoughts are not in order.

Just as definite changes occur in the body when thoughts are empowering and pleasurable.

Our thoughts are an unstoppable force that governs us. It is the reason for almost everything in our lives: wealth, poverty, sickness and health, love, loss, and happiness. This is the idea that our thoughts, feelings, and experiences create our life. It is often referred to as a universal law because what happens to us meets the requirements of our thoughts every time.

If you're like most people, you probably wouldn't consider yourself a 'law of attraction' person. You may say that you don't believe in all that new age mumbo jumbo or even perhaps take a professional and scientific approach to your daily life.

Interestingly, you experience the 'law of attraction' in your daily life regardless of how it happens. Even if you do not understand or believe in its existence, your thoughts, feelings, and behaviors manifest in your life.

Do you understand how cell service works? But you likely use your mobile phone daily, and it works for you regardless.

You can't think of something without it affecting you or someone else. When we think of how much we dislike our current job and can't wait to leave it, we take ourselves out of the present and attract what we don't want, which is a change in employment. Happiness is a choice as it is a state of mind. We can manifest positive or negative experiences in our life. If your life isn't what you want it to be. Then change your mind, and it will change your life.

We can manifest peace of mind by making the law of attraction work for us rather than against us. We can say NO to those thoughts we don't like and YES to those we do. We can refuse to think about someone who has hurt us by saying 'stop' to negative thoughts about them.

Let's start with a straightforward exercise that has immediate results: write down your frustrations and reframe them. Let me explain.

This is a modified version of cognitive behavioral therapy. Writing down your frustrations will help you solve them. It is a way of focusing your energy and effort on the problem. Whenever you're stressed, get a piece of paper or your computer, and write down exactly what's bothering you.

Now look at what you wrote and ask why you want to eliminate this. For example, if you wrote, 'my boss is a lazy jerk, and I just want to get out of here,' it may be true that your boss is pushing much work on you. However, look at the bigger picture and consider that maybe there are some excellent aspects to this job; write down the things you like about it.

You can consider how working with an uncooperative boss teaches you to be tactical and patient. It also allows you to learn and grow as you get work assigned to you that is the responsibility of someone higher up. You can think of what you have learned and have been able to accomplish that has been impressive. Consider the people in the company that you like to work with. Write it all down.

This will give you a clear idea of the pros and cons. Consider whether the 'pros' enjoyment outweighs the one issue you've been frustrated about. After using this exercise, when you're frustrated at something you are faced with regularly, you will begin to go through these steps instinctively in your mind, allowing you to minimize the effects of those things that cause frustration.

Whenever feelings of self-doubt, anger, and stress come around, simply write them down. Write down what you're frustrated about, then put your optimistic hat on, spin everything with a positive twist and write them down too. Things will become more evident, and some may vanish.

Another concept I want you to consider when you're frustrated is whether or not you can change the situation. Situations that cannot be changed are not worth your energy. Complaining or thinking negatively about something that will not change or has happened in the past and is not likely to reoccur will leave you even more frustrated. Recognize when you're feeling frustrated about things you cannot change and know that it's simply a situation you don't like, and that's okay. It happens in life. We are going to have conditions we don't like. Life isn't perfect. Know that you can't change it, and it isn't worth your energy. Then focus your energy on things you can change and enjoy. Complaining about things that cannot change provides nothing to you beneficial.

Driving home from my office, I hit every light, and it took me forever to get home, which I hadn't anticipated. This made me late for a conference call I had scheduled. Well, what am I going to do about that? It's over, and I can't change it. So there's no point in complaining about it, or dwelling on it, which will only raise cortisol levels and make me even more stressed. Just move on.

The Law of Attraction, the power of positive thinking, the power of prayer, and even science are some of the many different explanations as to why your thoughts and beliefs manifest. If you're feeling low or sad, you can take a little mental break by looking at all the fabulous possibilities in the world or some of your happiest memories. Thinking of something positive will make you more content at the moment and excited about what's ahead. It can be used as a kind of therapy. When we think deeply and effectively, we find solutions easier than when we only believe superficially about what's bothering us.

Re-affirming Courage

Affirmations are a straightforward and effective way of improving your life. Whenever you feel anxious, nervous, or afraid, your thoughts manifest in the world around you. You have created energy in which you are thinking about fear.

Instead of focusing on your worries, keep repeating to yourself that you're courageous. Say, 'I am brave' or 'I am strong,' and picture yourself using courage to overcome your fears. Remember a time when you were courageous and how it made you feel.

When anxious, say empowering affirmations out loud 30 times in a row. Hearing your claims aloud will give them more power. Whenever you are expressing an affirmation, use all three modalities to cement your thought: auditory, visual, and kinesthetic. Sound, sight, and emotions, if possible.

How do you incorporate visual stimulation in affirmations? You look in the mirror and smile! And you've got to feel the words you're saying. The more emotion and sense you experience, the more planted seeds in your subconscious mind.

The subconscious mind is more powerful than the conscious mind, so affirmations will get to our subconscious and eventually manifest themselves into reality. You can use them to plant the seeds you want to be planted and dig up unwanted seeds planted in the past. There are even other ways to use affirmations by adding them to visualization. If you're feeling down or sad, think of your favorite color and imagine yourself lying in a field of flowers that are all your favorite colors. If you're feeling nervous and excited, imagine yourself surrounded by positive thoughts and feelings. Focus on how these heightened emotions will help you overcome negativity.

Find a theme song and sing it out loud and to yourself when appropriate. Those empowering words feel good and create a garden of hope and opportunity.

Self-affirmations are a great way to improve our lives and make us feel confident. For example, 'I have all the resources I need to solve any problem.' Repeat these words until you believe in them and say them out loud, especially when feeling down or unconfident.

I like to find different ways of saying the same thing and having to consciously think about the meaning of the words you're speaking with emotion. This significantly impacts your subconscious mind.

Visualization

Visualization is the process of imagining a situation in your mind. You can either relive a negative or positive experience or construct a future occasion. It's not constructive to relive negative experiences unless you are doing so to learn from them. Visualizing positive memories are helpful at any time. But to manifest the future, visualize a situation or experience you want to occur. It would be best to imagine yourself experiencing your wish being fulfilled with all applicable emotions.

Let's say that there are many things you want to happen in your life. You want to earn more money, have a better relationship, and be healthier. You can make these things come true by visualizing them and believing they will come true.

Do you know how it reflects on your windshield when you place something on your car's dashboard? I've been obese in the past and weighed over 200 pounds. I knew this was extremely unhealthy, so I began working on my subconscious mind to develop a thin person's self-image.

I placed a picture of a woman in a bikini on my dashboard and told myself that it was me. And as I drove, my subconscious saw that photo repeatedly. I'd consciously say, 'you look fabulous and healthy today.'

If you want to earn more money, imagine getting that promotion or raise, picture yourself enjoying the lifestyle you will have once you make that much, and feel what it would be like to be even more successful than you already are. Feel the happiness and excitement it would bring into your life and the kind of people you will meet when you're more successful.

If you're having marital problems, visualize yourself in the best relationship with your spouse. Imagine how it would feel to fall in love all over again and have a healthy, happy relationship.

Visualize whatever you want, add in your emotions, and you will plant the seeds to make it happen! You can manifest anything into reality by harnessing the energy of your visions, thoughts, and feelings. You can change your life for the better by focusing on what's important to you and creating a picture with all the emotions of what you wish to accomplish. It's easy to do when you want something different for your life. And candidly, it makes you feel pretty good when you do it.

I authored a book, "*A Guide to Self Mastery.*" It is an instruction manual for meditation, mindfulness, thought control, and visualization. It's a three to five-month course that will change your life. If you're struggling with visualization, mindfulness, meditation, or controlling your thoughts, you can learn step by step how to implement these fantastic tools into your life: www.amazon.com/dp/B0BL418P63

Journal Your Thoughts

There's more benefit to journaling than just being able to express your feelings. Journaling is a creative way to harness the energy of your thoughts and turn them into something useful for yourself. Why don't we use journaling to write down a list of our goals? A list of the emotions we wish to feel today?

Our journal can also be used to brainstorm solutions for everyday problems, such as what career path we should take or how to deal with relationship issues. It's also an excellent place to develop creative ideas and inspirations we would otherwise not consider.

If we want our lives to be more successful and productive, we must consider more than just our superficial needs and wishes. We also need to think deeply about what stands in our way before they manifest into reality.

Have you ever noticed how therapists tend to ask their patients many questions? They give them time to think and let their minds drift around until they arrive at an answer that may initially seem irrational but is part of some deep-seated problem. We can do the same when solving our problems, such as finding a career we love or a job we want.

We will eventually solve any problem if we allow our minds to think clearly and deeply about what's troubling us and what we want for an outcome. Our thoughts guide our lives and other people's lives, so we need to think in the best way we can imagine.

Achieving mental clarity is a skill that must be developed and practiced over time if we want to move past our current circumstances and find solutions for the future. Our minds are mirrors that reflect our inner world, so the more we understand them, the more precise our vision will look when it's manifested into a reality.

The world is constantly changing and evolving, but we remain human beings with the same needs, interests, thoughts, and emotions. Applying these methods of practicing mindfulness will improve your life in many ways. It'll help you overcome problems before they manifest into reality and reach your goals faster and more proficiently.

By using manifestation and mindfulness, you can achieve your dreams faster, easier, and more efficiently than ever.

Passion is Key

Can you manifest something, goals, or dreams if you don't have a strong passion? Of course not. Missing passion can be a stumbling block in manifesting things into reality. The reason why different people manifest different things in their lives is that they each have unique passions and unique traits that are specific to them. If we don't love something, we won't do it as well as those who genuinely love whatever it is they're doing, so the manifestation of a goal will be much more easily achieved by someone who loves what they are trying to manifest.

Passion shows conviction. The subconscious mind doesn't know the difference between fiction and reality, but it does see the difference between thoughts and visions that lack emotion and passion versus those that are abundant.

Perhaps you're familiar with the famous quote by George Burns, *"I'd rather be a failure at something I love than succeed at something I hate."* This is a powerful statement because it supports my point that we need passion to manifest things into reality. It's much easier to achieve your dreams of big goals if you enjoy the journey.

However, I want to point out that you don't have to have specifics about what you're manifesting. For example, if you're having financial challenges and you visualize what your life would be like without them. That's where you start. Then you must also be observant in life; being mindful helps immensely with this. There will be a door that opens for you that will lead you to a way to achieve your vision. When the door opens, you must walk through it.

So, how can we apply passion while manifesting our goals? First, it must be in our visions. Second, we must take action and do things associated with what we want. For instance, if you want to become an entrepreneur, start by reading articles about entrepreneurship, watching videos about entrepreneurs, and listening to podcasts about how successful people started their businesses. Take every opportunity you can get to learn more about it.

Another approach is to start acting like the part. If you begin to act like an entrepreneur, it will only be a matter of time before reality catches up.

I have worked with many overweight and obese patients in my weight loss clinic, and it sounds simple, but the easiest way to lose weight is to start acting like a thin person. It will only be a matter of time before you'll become thin.

Leave a Review!

I would be incredibly thankful if you would take just 60 seconds to write a brief review on Amazon, even if it's just a few sentences.

tinyurl.com/MHMP-Review

Seeking Help

Chapter 10

Mental health conditions such as stress, anxiety, fear, depression, post-traumatic stress disorder (PTSD), bipolar and schizophrenia are complex and can often be challenging to discuss with others. Many people do not feel that they can be honest about these issues. As a result, many avoid seeking professional help and suffer in silence. This can lead to even more detrimental effects. Unfortunately, 37.2% do not seek professional help because they can't afford the cost, and 31.0% push it aside, assuming they can handle it.[19] It's almost as if these individuals think they are 'fighting' this problem independently and fall short of acknowledging that they need help.

It's imperative to accept and love yourself to get the help you need. Mental health is the state of someone's mind. This can include their ability to think clearly, solve problems, feel happy and content, go about everyday life, and manage stressful situations. It can also include depression; anxiety disorders, such as generalized anxiety disorder; substance abuse disorders, like alcoholism and drug addiction; eating disorders, such as anorexia nervosa and bulimia nervosa; schizophrenia; and other psychotic illnesses, such as dementia or delirium.

When to Seek Professional Help

At what point in life do you need professional help? If you're having thoughts of suicide, immediate assistance is required. It's vital that you get professional service immediately.

When you suspect recovery is probable and the thoughts are not severe or frequent enough to warrant an emergency call for assistance. Working through some of the practices described here might be beneficial before needing professional help.

If you feel that you aren't going in the right direction with your thoughts or that you don't feel you can get out of your current negative mental state without professional intervention, then it is time to reach out without delay.

Labeling yourself as 'sick,' 'weak,' or 'unstable' to cope with problems is not necessary or beneficial. It's essential to learn how to manage your thoughts and feelings effectively regardless of whether you seek professional guidance.

After Being Diagnosed with a Medical Condition

While doctors may be able to provide information about coping skills, most aren't trained in psychological therapy and self-help techniques. Medication helps to manage symptoms but cannot replace your relationship with a therapist. A therapist can help discuss ways to manage the condition and provide coping skills. They can also investigate the root cause of the situation, which is often related to psychological issues.

After the Death of a Loved One

This can affect anyone, but some people find it difficult to cope after a family member's death, especially when unexpected. Among other things, this can cause anxiety and stress, fear, and anger. You must express your emotions and discuss them to come to terms with what happened and learn from them when possible. Talking about the event helps with the grieving process and will give you back control over your emotions.

If You're Unable to Cope with Your Emotions

If you feel overwhelmed by your emotions, a therapist can help. They can talk through your feelings with you and provide techniques that allow you to move on from difficult or sad times in life. This can be important, especially if you're having thoughts about suicide. Emotions and thoughts about suicide can be different for everyone. They may range from mild sadness to anger. You may have thoughts of 'how could this happen?' or 'I can't deal with this any longer.' A therapist can help you manage these emotions and manage them healthily. They can also help you develop healthy ways to cope.

When You Can't Concentrate

A lack of concentration can signify other issues that need addressing. This can range from stress and anxiety to depression and low self-esteem. It's vital that you can concentrate on work and everyday tasks effectively. When your mind is elsewhere, it's challenging to do this. Discussing these issues with a therapist allows them to help you solve them. As well as providing coping skills, a therapist can help you identify the root cause.

If you're finding it difficult to concentrate or perform at work or school because of your emotions, it's a good idea to seek out professional help. This can be particularly important if your performance suffers from these issues. You may even be aware of this and want to resolve it but not know where to start. A therapist can help you with this and provide techniques to manage these emotions.

Other Times

You know it's time to seek help when you're having thoughts about suicide, if you're not coping with your emotions, or if you can't concentrate. What about when you feel something is wrong but aren't sure what it is? If it affects your everyday life, it might be time to seek support from a professional. A counselor can help by listening to what's going on in your life and helping identify the source. A therapist may be able to provide breathing techniques or other techniques that can help you unwind and relax. They will also be able to provide additional insight into issues that affect you.

Social Support

Getting support varies from discussions with family members or friends to needing professional help from a qualified therapist. Getting support and following some of the practices you have learned will make the process of becoming or maintaining mental health easier and get you on the path of wellness more efficiently.

Consider which source of support is best for you at this time.

Your Doctor

You can always approach your doctor to discuss any mental health issues that you may be having. Candidly, I feel this is the least effective support because most doctors aren't trained to help and don't know you well enough to offer appropriate advice. However, if you feel comfortable with your doctor, talking with them won't hurt and will likely lead to a good counselor or therapist recommendation, if nothing else.

Friends

Friends can be a source of support, but they are not trained to deal with mental health issues. Friends can help you develop coping skills, manage anxiety and stress, or identify negative thoughts. They also know you well and care about you, so any advice they give will likely be beneficial.

Therapy

A therapist can talk about your thoughts, feelings, and emotions non-judgmentally. They can also identify the root cause, which is vital when looking for a long-term solution. This may be different from what you think, so it's essential that you speak with someone qualified enough to know how to help you. When speaking with a therapist, you must feel comfortable talking about how you're feeling and what issues are affecting your life; otherwise, they will not be able to help as effectively.

A therapist also has skills in providing support and education that can help you to develop coping strategies. They can be a great source of reassurance when things aren't going well. You must feel comfortable and at ease with your therapist so that they can provide the most effective therapy possible.

Local Charities and Religious Counselors

Other options are available if you're uncomfortable speaking with a therapist or can't afford one. These may include local charities that provide free support to those suffering from mental health disorders. You can also speak with local religious counselors trained in helping people deal with emotions.

After reviewing these reasons to seek therapy and the alternatives available for social support you decide professional help isn't necessary at this time. You're welcome to skip the balance of this chapter. However, if it seems a therapist is your best option, I have some helpful information for you.

When You Choose a Therapist

Even though therapists are trained to help you, they're not clairvoyant. They can't read your mind and know exactly what it is that's affecting you. This is why you must be open and honest when speaking with them. When you're dishonest with your therapist, they will be unable to help you do what's right for you and assist in your recovery.

These are some things you can do to ensure that the therapy session will be as successful as possible.

Find the Right Therapist

It's essential that you find the right therapist for you. You must be comfortable talking to them, and they should have experience in dealing with similar issues as yours. This can help them provide effective therapy for you and allow them to empathize with your issues.

Ask for recommendations from your doctor if you can't find anyone you're comfortable with. You can also look online to see what you can find. Plenty of forums allow you to post reviews of therapists and have them reviewed by others. This will enable you to get a better idea of who is available and what your options are for therapy.

Reviews will also allow you to see how other people's therapy sessions went, how effective the therapist was, and what they liked and disliked about the experience. This can be useful when looking for a therapist. It can also remind you not to settle for someone who doesn't tick all your boxes.

You may be afraid of seeking support because of how people look at you or what they say about you. One of the main reasons why it's crucial to seek therapy is to learn how to handle these emotions and overcome them. Self-perception must become more important than other people's perceptions.

Discuss Costs First

The average therapist charges between $60 and $120 for every therapy hour.[20] How relaxed will you be during the therapy session if you worry about how much you have to pay? If you have concerns about the advertised price, speak with the therapist. They will be able to tell you if the cost includes medication, how much discount they may be able to provide, and how else they can help you. If you're still concerned, ask for a personal payment plan to know what your money is being used for and when it needs to be paid.

Once the financial issues are sorted out, you can focus on getting the support you need - which matters most.

Tell the Therapist Everything

You must tell your therapist everything; otherwise, they won't be able to help as efficiently. You have to be honest and open with your therapist so that they can understand the issues affecting you and provide adequate support. They may not be able to focus on all your problems at once if you don't tell them what you're dealing with, so it's crucial that you are as honest as possible.

Don't be shy. Don't be embarrassed. Don't be ashamed. Speak up, speak out, and let the therapist know what you're experiencing. They must know what you need for them to provide the best therapy possible.

Return Regularly

Regular return visits are vital in providing effective therapy. It would be best if you saw your therapist at least once a month, as it can take a while for issues to improve; otherwise, your symptoms will stay the same or get worse over time. Your therapist can stick with you through the process and keep tabs on how things develop with regular appointments.

Schedule sessions that suit you. You have to weigh the pros and cons of each therapist's option. Some therapists are available for appointments weekly, and others monthly. Some therapists work with couples, while others only deal with individuals. It would be best to decide which suits you to get the support you need most effectively.

Benefits of Therapy

Many people are afraid of seeking out therapy. They may believe it will be too embarrassing, or they'll have to tell the therapist things they don't want to. In some cases, this may be true, but it shouldn't prevent you from getting help. The benefits of mental health counseling make the process worthwhile, especially if you're getting therapy for anxiety issues.

Help with Personal Empowerment

Anxiety issues can prevent you from achieving your goals. They can make it hard to do things you would otherwise be able to do because they cause you to feel unsafe and uncomfortable. Anxiety can also get in the way of your relationships. Therapy sessions can help you overcome these issues and feel much more empowered when dealing with life's challenges.

Seeking help is the first step to taking control of your mental health issues. The sooner you do so, the sooner you can start taking control of your life and make the most of what it offers.

Improved Mood

Therapy sessions can help you feel calmer, happier, and more confident. With anxiety issues, it's often difficult to feel like you could tackle anything; but with therapy, this will start to change. With treatment, you'll learn how to manage the symptoms of your anxiety by learning how to deal with them positively.

Seventy-five percent of people who get therapy for their mental health report that they become happier once they start receiving treatment.[21]

Better Relationships

Your relationships can suffer if you don't get the support you need. Anxiety is one of the main reasons why people struggle to maintain relationships and make new ones. Suppose you're in a relationship but feel like it's becoming stressed because of your emotions, or you cannot control negative thoughts. In that case, therapy is essential to save that relationship. You'll learn how to be a better partner while improving your well-being with treatment. This creates a win-win situation that improves both yourself and your relationship without causing either side any harm or stress.

Techniques Therapists Use

Familiarizing yourself with your therapist's techniques should give you peace of mind. This helps you understand the process better and how it works. It'll also help you feel more confident about attending sessions, knowing you're in a safe and supportive environment.

Just by talking about your issues, you'll be able to discover things about yourself that you can't usually access on your own. A therapist will help you to come up with methods of dealing with feelings in a way that's suitable for you. You may find that the problems in your life sink or take on a different dimension when viewed through psychotherapy.

Therapy can also help solve relationship issues, improve self-esteem and reduce anxiety. In particular, psychodynamic therapy aims to achieve insight into the unconscious issues and motivations behind human behavior and problem-solving.

The therapist may have a relatively good idea of what you're going through, making them an excellent source for finding solutions. When looking at your case based on the information you've given them, they might even have suggested some solutions to others before, and they can review those theories with you.

Cognitive Behavioral Therapy (CBT) is a form of therapy that aims to help people solve problems and reduce anxiety. It shifts how the person thinks about their situation and how they react to it. With CBT, you'll look at yourself differently since you'll aim to change your thinking.

For example, if you're worried about an upcoming exam or presentation, CBT will aim to get you to concentrate on taking notes so that you don't panic as much as you would otherwise. While this might not always be possible for every situation, it can help many.

The therapy aims to make you more aware of the things that might cause you to feel anxious and give you the tools you need to deal with them. This helps to relax your mind so that you can think more clearly and work out what needs addressing to feel better about your situation.

The therapist will first explain how CBT works; then, they'll help guide you through a series of questions and exercises designed to help improve your thoughts about yourself and others.

Psychotherapy is the first line of defense against the problems that get in the way of people's lives. It's a unique solution that can help you to overcome high-stress situations or to address negative emotions and find relief from them. It's a way to get into your head, where you can make sense of the thoughts and feelings that run through it. It helps you to untangle your life by enabling you to understand what aspects of it need sorting out and what aspects are just part of the scenery.

Conclusion

We've addressed much in these several hours or days, and I'm hopeful that you are beginning to see the world in a different light. Maybe your blinders have been removed or at least been opened.

We all are at different places in this life journey, and I'm optimistic that your future will be more enjoyable and fulfilling than you had expected. If, while reading this book, you did so with optimistic expectations that the material and practices I've shared will work for you instead of doubting everything I have shared, then you have planted many seeds in your subconscious mind.

Optimistic expectations certainly would plant some seeds that will help you overcome anxiety, stress, and other deconstructive emotions.

When I was 26 years old, I got married, pregnant, and separated in only four months. Looking back on it, I saw all of the signs that this man was too good to be true, and immediately after we wed, I could see I was right.

Soon to become a single mom, I needed to change jobs because my job at the time required regular traveling, and that would quickly be out of the question. In addition to all of this, I had another battle to fight. All the debt we accumulated was in my name, including the cost of my wedding ring, as I later found out, and I had less than $100 to my name. I couldn't see the light at the end of the tunnel, and I did what I had never imagined I would do and filed for bankruptcy.

Many people talked to me about aborting my child because they could see my difficult situation, but I refused to see it. I had to reframe my thoughts many times. It's the first time in my life that I took up a theme song: *Break my Stride* by Matthew Wilder. The chorus went like this:

Ain't nothin' gonna break my stride
Nobody gonna slow me down
Oh no, oh no, I got to keep on moving
Ain't nothin' gonna break my stride
I'm running and I won't touch ground
Oh no, I got to keep on moving

This song was so upbeat that it was impossible to allow a negative thought to remain in my mind when I began to sing it. I didn't know how at the time, but I kept focusing on how my child and I would have a fabulous home, and we would be happy together.

I am amazed at how well I could keep the negative thoughts from consuming me. I simply pretended that everything was going to work out. I wanted to be a mother, and this is how life gave me what I wanted, so I was determined to make the best of it.

Although I had no idea how things would work out, I just knew that the pain of thinking of everything negatively was too much for me to handle, so I'd make sure that every time a negative thought would pop into my mind, I'd have it erased, like an eraser on a chalkboard. I'd immediately turn my attention to the vision I created of my child living comfortably in my beautiful future home with me.

Image what happened. As I looked through the want ads, I found an advertisement for a new home salesperson. It indicated that no experience was needed, which was good because I didn't have any. Before the interview, I borrowed a book about selling and studied it repeatedly. I had been selling a little, but candidly, I wasn't a master, and it was a service to businesses. This book had techniques I could apply to sell anything, including homes.

I interviewed with human resources first and went through to the final interview with the president. She hired me on the spot. It was the start of a twenty-eight-year career in the industry that not only I enjoyed but paid me handsomely. My mother used to tell me that God smiled at me the day I saw that want ad. All of this happened because

I focused on my mental health and wouldn't allow myself to accept or dwell on the negative aspects of my situation.

Do you believe this would have happened if I had taken an alternative approach to my thoughts? If I had a pity party with myself daily and made different decisions that were a result of all the adverse events in my life at the time?

My life was turned upside down, inside out, and somehow, someway, I landed on top. This chain of events turned out to be the best thing that ever happened to me. My son is my only child. And the career and courage I developed changed my life.

Our world has been created in our minds and can be changed there too. You control your thoughts, which become beliefs, and your beliefs have faith and manifest into your world. You, indeed, are the master of your destiny.

Although there may be times when our mental health prevents us from experiencing all of the wonders life has to offer, the mind is a miracle that can be altered and changed and is a tool you can use to create the life you want and can enjoy.

By giving your energy to positive, constructive thoughts rather than negative, destructive thoughts, you can enjoy every moment more fully and construct the future of your dreams.

> *"Faith is the substance of things hoped for, the evidence of things not seen."*
>
> Hebrews 11:1 King James Version

I want to leave you with this last thought about faith. Thoughts without faith don't have the impact of faithful thoughts. You can tell yourself all day long that you're 29 years old when you're 59 and won't ever become it because you KNOW it's not true and never will be.

But let's use something a little more realistic; faith can be shown when a married couple decides to have a child. And they begin to try, but simultaneously, they convert the office into a nursery and begin to decorate it. They also start to buy clothes for their infant that will be coming soon. She's not pregnant yet. No. She's not, but they know the child is coming.

One way or another, this couple will have a child even if they adopt.

On the other hand, they could keep their study as is; the wife can change careers while trying. Which couple would you bet money on getting a child? Darn right, I'd be betting on couple number one. They are expecting a child, whether she's pregnant or not. That's faith.

Faith is an energy that permeates everything and everyone. It's when you believe in something so firmly that you bring it to reality. Everything around you is energy. There is nothing solid in this life; it's just vibrating electrons and atoms that form something that appears solid because their vibration is in harmony with the others around it.

Think about our mobile phones once again. We can talk to someone on the other side of the world because of energy. Energy has impressive power, and faith is one of those energies. Your thoughts and beliefs are as well. And just as your voice can travel halfway around the world through an energy force, so can your thoughts. Thoughts with faith find a way, and they will find a way to help you achieve your beliefs.

You may simply want to feel better daily and enjoy each moment with more happiness, less stress, and less anxiety. You may want to declutter the mind and feel pleasure more often. Candidly, those are relatively easy goals to accomplish if you take action with the magnificent power of thought.

On the other hand, you can take this further and begin to construct a future. I could have never imagined that I would have been able to do and accomplish what I have in life. No one in my family had been on a plane the day I took my first flight when I was 19 years old. Yet today, I have traveled to most of the United States, Europe, South America, some of the Middle East, and more. If I had lived in the world I was born instead of the world I created (or, I like to say, co-created), none of that would have happened.

You can choose to be happy and to achieve more regardless of your past, and it all starts with mental health or, should I say mental peace. Begin to imagine constructive, optimistic thoughts. Plant a healthy garden to flourish into the most beautiful thing you've ever seen—one thought at a time.

Just for You!

A FREE GIFT FOR OUR READERS

Get my free eBook on sweeteners...the good, the bad and the ugly. Which sweeteners to avoid and which provide health benefits.

Visit *www.tamgall.com/sweeteners-ebook*

Resources

1. Charles F. Haanel. (2020, June 26). *The History of The Master Key System and Its Influence | Charles F. Haanel. Charles F. Haanel | the Man Who Unlocked the World, the Author of the Master Key System, and the Father of Personal Development*. Retrieved October 12, 2022, from https://www.haanel.com/history-influence/

2. Hopkins, T. (1982, September 29). *The Official Guide to Success, V. 1: Tom Hopkins' Personal Success Program*. Hopkins.

3. Wikipedia contributors. (2022, September 27). *Enteric nervous system*. Wikipedia. Retrieved October 12, 2022, from https://en.wikipedia.org/wiki/Enteric_nervous_system

4. Woo, C. (2021, October 15). *Our second brain: More than a gut feeling*. UBC Neuroscience. Retrieved October 12, 2022, from https://neuroscience.ubc.ca/our-second-brain-more-than-a-gut-feeling/

5. Hopkins, T. (1982, September 29). *The Official Guide to Success, V. 1: Tom Hopkins' Personal Success Program*. Hopkins.

6. Abraham, Hicks, J., & Hicks, J. (2004). *Ask and it is Given: Learning to Manifest Your Desires.* Penguin Random House.

7. Vasković, J., MD. (2022, July 6). *Celiac plexus.* Kenhub. Retrieved October 15, 2022, from https://www.kenhub.com/en/library/anatomy/celiac-plexus

8. Kristin. (2022, August 24). *How to Heal & Open Your Solar Plexus Chakra.* Be My Travel Muse. Retrieved October 15, 2022, from https://www.bemytravelmuse.com/solar-plexus-chakra/

9. Bryant, C. (n.d.). *The relationship between attitudes to aging and physical and mental health in older adults | International Psychogeriatrics.* Cambridge Core. Retrieved October 15, 2022, from https://www.cambridge.org/core/journals/international-psychogeriatrics/article/abs/relationship-between-attitudes-to-aging-and-physical-and-mental-health-in-older-adults/5824A4FC3E98C7DD65F6A4BC0E68E98F

10. *Stress, Anxiety and Your Immune System: How to Avoid Getting Sick | Hartford HealthCare | CT.* (n.d.). Retrieved October 16, 2022, from

https://hartfordhealthcare.org/about-us/news-press/news-detail?articleId=18853

11. Cook, G. (2016, January 19). *The Science of Healing Thoughts*. Scientific American. https://www.scientificamerican.com/article/the-science-of-healing-thoughts/

12. O'Connell, C. (2021, April 16). *Quantum physics for the terminally confused*. Cosmos. https://cosmosmagazine.com/science/physics/quantum-physics-for-the-terminally-confused/

13. Charles F. Haanel. (2021, November 24). In *Wikipedia*. https://en.wikipedia.org/wiki/Charles_F._Haanel

A Guide to Self-Mastery

Change Your Life by
Changing Your Thoughts
Through the Law of Attraction,
Master Key System,
Mindfulness,
Meditation and
Visualization

Tammy Gallagher

Author's Preface

Imagine for a moment that your perspective is just an inkling of the accurate makeup of the truth. Imagine you have unlimited resources and the power to create anything and everything you desire. Imagine that you control every situation or circumstance in your life, and nothing is beyond your control.

Now stop imagining... and believe!

This is a factual truth and the potential you have been empowered with. This is, in effect, what has created your reality and will continue to create your reality.

What is it that you want out of life? Health, love, money? You can have all these things. The world often refers to this process as the *Law of Attraction*. You must train your mind to create the proper thoughts and visions, and the seed of thought will be planted and grow into a belief that will ultimately deliver to you the circumstance consistent with your heart's desires. It sounds simple. Well, here's the story...

Scientists often state that we use only about ten percent of our brain's capacity. Have you ever wondered what you could achieve using one hundred percent of your brain's ability? Many consider *The Master Key System*, written by Charles F. Haanel, the key to opening that door.

Haanel wrote several books published by Psychology Publishing and his Master Key Institute. In addition to *The Master Key System*, which he wrote in 1912, he also wrote *Mental Chemistry* and *The New Psychology*.[1]

By 1933, *The Master Key System* had sold more than 200,000 copies and seemingly vanished. It resurfaced many years later.[1] This system teaches the ultimate principles, causes, effects, and laws that bring about all achievement and success. It is said that *The Master Key System* shows you how to get what you want in life. My experience with *The Master Key System* has been amazing!

In November 2006, I began studying with a good friend. If I recall correctly, this is about when the documentary, *The Secret*, came out. We had a weekly master mind meeting, during which we explored universal laws and related them to our beliefs. It was at this time that we began to study the *Master Key*.

Although *The Master Key System* seemed profound and impactful, it was a challenging read and outdated. Not only did it need to be updated with current terminology, but life has progressed since the early 1900s, and much of what was written was challenging to relate to. Despite these things, I continued to review the first two lessons repeatedly. Something inside me told me I needed to go through all twenty-four lessons. I was inspired to begin re-writing each lesson in my own words in simple, easy-to-read terminology that applied to today's world. By doing this, I not only created *The Guide to Self-Mastery* but also was able to plant the seeds of thought that grew into an unconscious understanding of the teachings.

I found that changing the way I thought and prayed allowed me to realize the extent to which God is within me and how He wants me to succeed more than I can imagine. This new way of using my mental power allowed me to expand my mind and feel more in sync with God and the Universe in ways I never thought possible.

This information will open your mind and allow you to realize the unlimited possibilities that are within your reach, and how to use your connection with Eternal Energy to construct the life you've always wanted.

The Master Key System sets out the fundamental principles of life and creative living as Haanel understood and applied them. *The Guide to Self Mastery* is my interpretation of Charles Haanel's original writings. Essential to his teaching is the proper development and use of mental power – the key to genuinely creative power and action, harmony and health, love and happiness, and abundant possibilities.

To effectively integrate the teachings of *The Guide to Self-Mastery* into your life, it is essential that you commit to three to five months of study and practice. There are no shortcuts here. Reading *The Guide to Self-Mastery* like a novel from cover to cover will give you some benefits, but to transform your life and make your new way of thinking an unconscious habit, make the three to five-month commitment. It will only take about thirty minutes each day, and the reward will be significant.

Each chapter represents four to seven days of study. You must read, re-read and listen to each chapter multiple times and complete the appropriate chapter meditation exercises consistently and regularly during the four to seven days to master each lesson. You move on to the next chapter and meditation exercise when you strongly understand the prior chapter material and have mastered the chapter exercise.

In this book, I refer to God in many ways. The Infinite, the Divine, and the All-Powerful are just a few. God's spirit I refer to also in alternate ways, such as Universal Energy and Eternal Energy. God's intelligence and resources I often refer to as the Universal Mind. Ultimately, I believe in God. And if you believe in a higher power, a Creator, then feel free to substitute your beliefs within the scope of this book. My intention here is not to teach any religion but instead to teach universal laws, and it is up to you to put it into the context of your religion.

You are about to transform yourself, and it is a journey that will revolutionize how you think and renovate your core beliefs. Each step of the process prepares you for the next.

> *"... (it) is like driving at night in the fog. You can only see as far as your headlights, but you can make the whole trip that way."*
>
> *~Edgar Lawrence Doctorow, Author*

Embrace each week and focus on the study and meditation exercise within that week alone, and the transformation will unfold effortlessly. You'll be given step by step instructions to learn mindfulness, meditation, creative visualization, and more.

You are about to start a journey to explore the power of the Divine within you, integrate your understanding of Supreme Law, master the *Law of Attraction*, and connect with the Universal Mind. You are about to start a journey that will change your life!

Introduction

It was December 26, 1989, the day I had hoped would be the happiest day of my life. I was getting married. I had dated my fiancé for only about six months, and my inner voice was telling me that I was rushing into this, but he kept moving up the date and had a sense of urgency that was unexplainable to me. Ignoring my gut feeling, I got married on that day.

Everything happened so quickly. We bought a home in January, and I was blessed and conceived in February.

As newlyweds, we needed things for our new home, we went on a beautiful honeymoon, and in addition to other things, we promptly accumulated debt. Between the two of us, I was the one with good credit, so this debt was in my name.

As quickly as all of this occurred, just as quickly it all fell apart. We were separated after only four months of marriage and divorced shortly after that. Soon to become a single mother, I changed jobs because I regularly traveled, which would quickly be out of the question.

In addition to becoming pregnant, separating, divorcing, and changing jobs to a commissioned position, I had another battle to fight. All the debt we had accumulated was in my name, including my wedding ring, which I later found out, and my now ex-husband was not taking responsibility for any of it. I had less than $100 to my name, and I couldn't see the light at the end of the tunnel. I did what I had never before imagined I would do and filed for bankruptcy.

Shortly after my son was born, he required an operation. It was a routine operation common in boys; however, this $14,000 operation was not within my finances. The court order requiring the father to carry medical insurance was ignored, as the father canceled my son's medical insurance. Add this to the significant amount of unpaid child support and the fact that the father moved away and hadn't seen his son since shortly after his birth; I decided it would be better if I controlled our destiny. I returned to court and gained full custody of my son.

My life was turned upside down, inside out, and somehow, someway, it was the best thing that had ever happened to me!

Let me explain...

During this process, I never once thought about aborting my son. I believed that he was meant for greatness. Why else would he have been given to me so quickly? Me... the one who couldn't possibly consider giving up a child. It was as if God knew that this soul was meant to be born, and that's why I had been chosen to be the mother.

Additionally, the thought that raising a child on my own would be difficult had never occurred to me. It didn't matter that my family wasn't local, and I didn't have much support. I knew I'd somehow be given what I needed when needed.

As a result of what most would consider a nightmare, not only was I blessed with an awesome son, but I found a career that was meant for me: a business that I love, that I'm good at, and that compensates well. When I was 'forced' to find another job, I took a position as a new home sales associate. Seventeen years later, I progressed from novice sales associate with no college degree to division president.

I ran a multimillion-dollar division of the world's most experienced home builder.

The entire journey was one of amazement when I looked back. For example, one of the minimum requirements of most positions I held since 1995 was a bachelor's degree in business or a related field. I didn't even complete my associate degree, much less a bachelor's.

Additionally, men predominantly run residential development due to the work involved. Not many women are in construction and development compared to men. Not only do I not have a degree, but upon my departure, I was the only female division president nationwide for this builder. What a fantastic experience and accomplishment that I never could have imagined!

Fast forward to 2015, and although there was much in between, the final position I held was senior vice president over a region of seven divisions. I don't share this with you to impress you, but to impress upon you that belief creates impressive results. This want ad for a new home salesperson with no experience needed appearing in front of me in 1990 ultimately led me to a 28-year career.

In the mid-1990s, when my career began to kick in high gear, I believed that much of what was occurring to me was good luck. I used to say that life planned my career better than I could have planned it myself.

I now know that I planned all of it. In 1990, when I first began to understand that my marriage wasn't going to last, I attached myself to the book *The Official Guide to Success* by Tom Hopkins. I was convinced that Hopkin's material, when applied, could significantly improve my results.

The Official Guide to Success became my 'sanity bible.' I learned, among other things, that if I 'faked it,' I'd make it.[2] It would all work out if I pretended to be the person I desired to be. It would only be a matter of time before I became that person. Anything, and everything, I could do to keep the fear, doubt, and worry out of my mind I did. And this book helped me tremendously.

I had a theme song that I sang whenever I began to feel down and felt like I was sliding into depression. Somehow, as I began to sing this uplifting song, it would bring me back to a happier state.

I additionally sang *You Are My Sunshine* to my son while rocking him to sleep. I knew he was such a blessing, and it would all work out if I stayed focused on my blessings.

The Official Guide to Success was the first book I read that focused on the power of positive thinking, the power within. This book proved to me that there is power in our thoughts. This is the book that started me on my journey that led to *A Guide to Self-Mastery*.

Instructions

Chapter Material

Most people will want to read this book like a novel, and although you may decide to do so, I suggest afterwards, you re-read the book in the following format.

There are five activities listed below, and I recommend that you complete every activity with each chapter before progressing to the next chapter. I also suggest that you complete a minimum of one activity per day and all five activities within the four-to-seven-day period for each lesson chapter.

- Read the chapter silently

- Read the chapter aloud
- Listen to the audio of the chapter
- Listen to the audio of the chapter while simultaneously silently reading the chapter
- Listen to the audio of the chapter while highlighting in the book or taking notes on the impactful messages

Exercises

Each chapter has a meditation exercise. It would be best if you invest fifteen to thirty minutes per day. All the meditation exercises will require you to select a room where you can be alone and undisturbed. This should be a place that is accessible daily. You'll be asked to sit erectly in a chair or on the ground, or lie on your back in your bed or on the ground or a mat. Select your room based on what's appropriate for your preferred position and one that will be available for a minimum of three to five months for the twenty-four-chapter lessons.

The first four exercises will ultimately bring you through the steps to meditation. Others describe this process as preparing yourself to receive the Holy Spirit in prayer. These exercises may be a refresher if you're used to meditating or praying in silence with only controlled thought.

Exercises five through twenty-four should start by bringing yourself to this meditative state. It is in meditation, when you inhibit uncontrolled thoughts and have control over your body and mind, where you connect with the Divine.

All exercises ask you to sit erect or lie comfortably on your back without lounging. If you're lying down, keep your feet apart about shoulder width or slightly closer with your feet comfortably open to the outside. Keep your hands at your sides with your palms down, or place one on your stomach and one on your heart. Your head and neck should be in alignment with your spine so that your spine through your head is level.

If you're sitting and are used to meditating, you may take your traditional meditative position. Otherwise, it is suggested that you sit comfortably on the floor with your legs crossed Indian style. If you prefer to sit on a chair, do so erectly with your feet flat on the floor. Do not cross your legs. In either case, place your hands on your legs or knees comfortably with your palms down. While sitting, you can also bring your hands together if you prefer. Again, you want to keep your spine aligned with your neck and head.

Keeping your spine, neck, and head aligned allows for the most direct physical connection between your brain and gut. Your second brain is located in the gut. The gut-brain, known as the enteric nervous system, is a mass of nerves embedded in the walls of our gastrointestinal tract, most of which reside in the midsection or the gut.

The enteric nervous system can operate independently of the brain, which is why it's referred to as our second brain.[3] The vagus nerve connects the two brains, which is how they communicate. It's also believed that gut health can directly affect our mental health.[4] The phrase 'gut feeling' has some science to back it up.

Why is it essential to sit erect and keep the head, neck, and spine in alignment during meditation? Most will say that it helps with deep breathing, but from my experience, I'm convinced that this communication between both brains is enhanced and makes meditation more impactful.

Once you have identified the location and the physical position you intend to take during the meditation exercises, you must also ensure the proper environment. Do not have any noise in the background, with the exception of mellow instrumental music, if you prefer. Turn cellular phones off and any other items that could cause an interruption.

This is the environment, location, and position you will duplicate for every meditation exercise. Therefore, be sure to choose a room and position that will be appropriate and comfortable for all the meditations for up to twenty-four weeks and beyond.

Each meditation must be repeated six times before moving to the next chapter. You can complete the meditation exercise once or twice per day and continue the meditation until you have it mastered. You may progress to the next chapter only after learning the meditation exercise and developing a solid understanding of the chapter content. If completed correctly, this should take four to seven days per chapter.

Let's get started.

All Power Comes from Within

Chapter One

Do you ever notice that everything goes your way when you get on a roll? Or that the people who have everything seem to get even more? It's as if the wealthy get wealthier and the poor get poorer. The healthy never have to worry about their health, and the sick get sicker. What about those people who never seem to get a break?

Ultimately, we tend to get more of whatever we have going on in our lives, whether we like it or not. Why is this so? That's what we are going to explore, and if you understand this, then you should be able to change it at will, wouldn't you think?

Your reality is a reflection of your beliefs, and your beliefs are shaped by your conscious thought interpreting what you observe every day.

Suppose you knew failure wasn't possible and success was already guaranteed, that you had all the power of the most powerful, and the abundance of the most affluent. Would you be concerned about the outcome of any of your endeavors? Of course not. So, imagine that you have all of that. What would you do? What would be possible? What would you change? How would you act on your inspiration?

The incredible reality is that you already have this power. It's already within you, and you are already using this power daily. If your present reality or circumstances are not what you desire, then you are not using this power effectively, and you are most likely not using this power consciously. So how do you use this power to get everything you desire?

The secret is as simple as learning how to think correctly. Really! You have two feelings, for the most part – pleasure and pain. They are both motivators. You want more joy and less pain. Everyone prefers to feel good versus bad, wouldn't you agree?

Have you ever had a day when everything went your way? It felt great. Did you feel great because everything went your way? Or did everything go your way because you felt great? The latter is likely the more accurate explanation of your fantastic day and every other day that you've considered phenomenal.

Your body and mind are united. They cannot live separate lives just as your physical and mental worlds are united. It is impossible for your physical world not to follow your mental world. Or another way to look at it is that your outer world follows your inner world.

There is no way for everything to go your way if you are in a horrible mood. Similarly, having a dreadful day is impossible when you have an optimistic attitude. Harmony in how you feel or your non-physical world will create harmony in your physical world.

In everything you accomplish, achieve, or becomes your reality, the following is true:

- You achieve only if you believe you can
- Your beliefs are consistent with who you are
- Who you are is shaped by what you think

What you think leads to whom you become, and what you become leads to what you achieve or attract into your life. But there's more to it than that because we must consider the entire Universe in this equation. This becomes more complicated to explain, but the result is still as simple as thoughts create your beliefs and create what you become, and your beliefs and who you have become create your expectations. In due course, your expectations create actions and circumstances consistent with your thoughts every time.

Wouldn't it be nice if, when you had a thought, everyone and everything in the Universe responded to your thoughts as if they were commands that must be followed?

Of course, that would be amazing! Not only would that be amazing, but that is the potential with which you have been empowered. Not in some future time and place, but right here, right now!

Do you believe in a Higher Power? Do you believe that our Higher Power, the Divine, is in each of us? There is no doubt in my mind. Science supports the miracle of life. This Universal Energy that unites us all has power. We are connected with the Divine through our subconscious mind, and we all have this connection.

The Divine, the Infinite, the Universal Mind or Energy, the Holy Spirit, the All-Powerful, the Universal Substance, and our Eternal Energy are words used to name God's magical, mysterious power. The Universal Mind is the life principle of every atom that exists. Every atom is intelligent and seeks to carry out the purpose for which it was created. It is All-Powerful, creative by nature, always present, and the powerful force behind our connectedness or oneness with all in the Universe. So, when you think consciously or subconsciously, you connect with everyone and everything in the Universe through your connection to the Universal Mind or the God within us. It is Omnipotent Law.

Most people live only in their physical or outer world, yet it is the non-physical spirit of the Universe within you that creates everything in the physical world.

The Universal Mind is not objective but subjective. It does not judge your beliefs and determine whether it will cooperate with you; this Universal Energy connects your beliefs to everyone and everything in the Universe so that you can deliver the result of your beliefs in your physical world.

Therefore, if you believe it, you will attain it, whether or not it is what you want. Everyone and everything in the Universe instinctively, without conscious thought, responds to your thoughts and beliefs and will provide you with an environment or situation consistent with your beliefs.

Each individual is a part of this Universal Energy. Universal Energy creates only through the individual, and the individual can create only through Universal Energy.

Correlating this for those who believe in God or Jesus Christ, the Holy Spirit within you connects with the Spirit within each of us. Some people say that God uses all of us to answer the prayers of others. He creates everything through the individuals.

The circumstances of situations that occur do so because of your thoughts. Let's look at an example, such as your body weight. Your weight today is a result of the behavior and actions of your recent past. Your recent behavior reflects your current beliefs resulting from your past thoughts. Ultimately, your past thoughts created the chain of events that resulted in your current weight.

However, if you decide today that you will lose weight and know that failure is not an option, you immediately begin to change your thoughts. The changes include how you think about your food intake and exercise, among other things. Your beliefs know that improvements in this regard will result in weight loss.

In this example, only after your behavior changes will the result begin to manifest physically. So if you start acting as if you're one hundred thirty pounds when you are two hundred pounds, you will eventually become one hundred thirty pounds. But if you continue to believe that you can't lose weight, this will affect your behavior, and change won't occur.

In The Official Guide to Success, Tom Hopkins says, "Fake it until you make it." [5] If you act like you're already where you want to be, the physical reality will follow.

In this analogy, your behavior in the physical world brings about the desired result. But what if you need others for the desired effect to be attained? What if you didn't know what to do to achieve the desired result? The good news is that the same approach still works. Your connection with Universal Energy will help you find your way.

Your thoughts will shape your beliefs, and your beliefs will attract the circumstances and situations in your physical world needed to bring about your desired result. However, what is most important to understand is that the energy of beliefs is All-Powerful and permeates everything and everyone in the Universe, not only your physical actions but also those of others.

By understanding this, you begin to partner with Universal Energy in designing your own life's reality. You co-create with the All-Mighty!

Every result or effect in your outer world has been caused by your thoughts and orchestrated through Universal Energy. When you believe something, you are in direct alignment with attracting it. Your beliefs connect with the Universe through Universal Energy, which permeates everything and everyone. This mental action and reaction are the *Law of Causation*.

So, imagine that it will become if you think it, believe it, and expect it. There is a difference between hoping for something and knowing it will result. Using the weight loss example again, when you decide that you will accomplish your weight-loss goal, and you know that nothing will prevent you from achieving it, when you genuinely know and expect it as sure as the sun rising in the morning, then you attain it, don't you?

If you say, 'I'll try to lose weight' or 'I'll give it a shot,' that is permitting yourself to fail, and that is not the same as knowing you'll lose weight and likely will not achieve your goal. Your thoughts lack belief. You must have faith that your desired result is inevitable, or you will achieve what you know is certain.

Your physical world is observed through your senses and then interpreted by your conscious mind. Through your thoughts, your conscious mind makes conclusions about happenings, and the conclusions shape your beliefs. Once a belief is fully formed, it is stored in the subconscious mind. The subconscious doesn't make decisions about whether something is true or false or if something is right or wrong. The subconscious takes the conclusions of the conscious mind as fact.

When you observe through your senses and interpret things constructively, you build a constructive belief that your entire body feels. It feels good and results in a harmonious state in your physical and non-physical worlds. That belief is then deposited into the subconscious mind for future use.

If you interpret things as destructive, you build a harmful belief, which is also felt by your entire body. This doesn't feel good. It doesn't feel good because your emotions tell you that your interpretation was incorrect. The siren goes off because you exit the emergency exit door in error. Esther and Jerry Hicks, the authors of *Ask and It is Given*, call it your 'Emotional Guidance System.'[6] If you don't feel good, your Emotional Guidance System is telling you that you have misinterpreted things and are shaping the wrong beliefs, which will bring about the bad result or future reality.

How can two people observe the same things but interpret them differently? This is usually a result of their current beliefs. When you consciously control your thoughts, you shape your beliefs. Once a belief is accepted as fact it will ultimately instinctively be used by the subconscious mind and Universal Energy. Your beliefs connect with Universal Energy, which connects your beliefs to the entire Universe.

Suppose your subconscious mind communicates through Universal Energy to everyone and everything in the Universe. In that case, everyone unconsciously begins to rearrange their lives to create a circumstance consistent with your belief. Pretty compelling and impressive.

Your connection to Universal Energy is always powerful and present, whether you realize it or not. When you think, you activate the power of Universal Energy accordingly. Every thought, therefore, is the cause of a reaction. You think something, and Universal Energy begins to act through vibrations instantly, and there will eventually be a reaction accordingly. Because of this, it is essential that you control your thoughts as you prompt Universal Energy to work on your behalf and ultimately deliver to you the conditions that are in alignment with your thoughts.

There will always be a reaction to your thoughts every time. It is the only way you create anything in your life. It is the only way anything is made in the Universe. All power is under your control through your thoughts and beliefs. When you thoroughly understand this Omnipotent Law, you can apply it to all conditions, which is the basis for all physical things.

The non-physical eternal being that you are creates everything in the physical world. We live through our conscious thoughts and subconscious reactions, which are connected to everyone and everything in the Universe through Universal Energy or the Spirit within each of us.

Somehow we have been conditioned, and most of us today subconsciously believe, that the outer world has the solutions to change. The outer world is what creates opportunities for us and the circumstance we are living with today.

However, that is untrue. For example, if you are ill, medical care treats the symptoms or the physical cause of the illness. Omnipotent Law says that you must change the thinking and belief of the individual, and the physical world will respond accordingly. Without a change in belief, the medical solution will not cure the cause. But if you believe the medical solution will cure the cause, then and only then will it.

Remember, you already have this power, and it is always working. Your reality today is a result of your thoughts and beliefs. You have co-created your current reality with the cooperation of Universal Energy. It is that simple.

If you're unhappy with your current reality, you have deposited beliefs into your subconscious mind that are not aligned with your true desires. Therefore, you have used this power unintentionally to prevent you from attaining your true desires.

Listen to your 'Emotional Guidance System.' When you don't feel good about something, your thoughts are not aligned with what you want. That bad feeling is your siren warning you that your thoughts are communicating with Universal Energy and what ultimately will be delivered to you if you don't change course are circumstances that are not going to feel good.

The only way to maximize the power within to attract what you truly desire is in a harmonious state. Think about it... your weight-loss program won't work if you keep focusing on how it won't work or that you don't want to do what you've set out to do. When you focus on it not working, you don't feel great about starting your weight-loss program, do you? There's a conflict between your goal and your thoughts and beliefs; therefore, you're not in a harmonious state. Thus, there's no way that you'll be successful.

When you're mentally efficient, your thoughts feel good and align with your desired result. Your non-physical being is in a harmonious state. All is good. The more you can stay unified, the more you align with the Universe's forces that will bring you circumstances that are consistent with your desires.

How do you intentionally feel harmonious?

It's all about controlling your thoughts and interpreting everything with a positive spin so that you develop constructive beliefs that will work to your advantage versus your detriment. Have faith and know that the way you have decided to view the situation will be your truth and your reality.

The great news is that by applying Omnipotent Law, you can substitute any favorable situation for a negative one, abundance for poverty, wisdom for ignorance, pleasure for pain, and freedom for oppression. You can attract anything you desire and have the discipline to pursue.

Meditation Exercise One

This exercise aims to master securing control of your physical body. You must be able to control your body before you progress to the next chapter.

Take your position as described in the Introduction and relax. Inhale deeply, and exhale slowly. Feel your stomach rise with each inhale and fall as you exhale. Keep every other body part perfectly still. Let your thoughts roam where they will yet recognize your breathing and what it does to your body when you breathe deeply.

Do this for no less than ten minutes. Continue this once or twice daily for a minimum of four days or until you secure complete control of your physical body. You must master stillness and have a strong understanding of this chapter before progressing to the next chapter and exercise.

The Power of the Subconscious Mind

Chapter Two

Most know that our mind operates in two modes, consciously and subconsciously. The conscious mind deals with things in your outer world. It reasons and therefore has limited capacity and processes relatively slowly.

The subconscious mind deals with your inner world. It perceives by intuition and absolutes and processes rapidly. It has unlimited capacity due to its unity with the Divine. Our subconscious mind makes decisions so effectively and efficiently that it always makes the correct decision based upon the absolute guidelines it has been given to follow.

The conscious mind cannot function in the same manner as the subconscious. When you stop and think about something, this slows down the processing time. Imagine what would happen if we had to consciously make every decision associated with the operations of our vital organs. At our present conscious capacity, we could never be able to sustain our own lives.

We don't have time to think about whether it's time to take a breath or whether our heart should pump some blood right now.

Relying upon your conscious mind for all mental functions would be similar to depending upon a nut for your annual nourishment, yet most people attempt to do that today.

Your conscious mind doesn't have the capacity or power that the subconscious does. When comparing the conscious mind to the power of the subconscious, the subconscious is still very unexplainable and accomplishes incredible tasks and results. How the subconscious works is still a mystery.

The value that the subconscious mind provides is enormous. It is a warehouse of memories and facts, principles and dreams. It inspires us and instinctively directs us. It's artistic and creative and stores our ideals.

Physical, spiritual, and mental power all comes from our subconscious. The physical power the subconscious mind provides is its ability to operate vital processes, with the preservation of your physical life and all life, including restoration of health. Yes, that's correct! The physical power of the subconscious mind includes the ability to heal. This physical power is something within you that starts at conception. The competent cells within your body know how to heal, which is their natural state.

The spiritual power of the subconscious is the source of your dreams, aspirations, and imagination. It is united with the Divine, and the more we recognize our connection to the Divine, the more powerful our relationship becomes and the more we can use it for the benefit of ourselves and others.

The subconscious mind's mental power is the ability to memorize and store knowledge. It is what controls your initiative and stores your beliefs. It is the warehouse for your habits.

Your subconscious mind is always working, and it works with precision regularly. Everything that you do with ease and perfection is done through your subconscious. It is believed that it is through the subconscious that the most creative genius resides.

The physical power of your subconscious is the dimension that your conscious mind can significantly influence. Your subconscious mind acts as if all decisions and beliefs developed by the conscious mind are valid. It doesn't judge or question, as it doesn't have time for that. Like a perfect computer program, your subconscious mind processes based on how the program was written, and your conscious mind writes and re-writes the program. Therefore, what you believe to be accurate, your subconscious acts upon it as if it is true every time.

Think of all the things we do without thought – walking, blinking, digesting, breathing, etc. We use our five senses without thinking about how we process what we see, feel, hear, touch and smell. We would have difficulty consciously stopping some of the things our subconscious routinely operates. Have you tried to stop your heart from beating or your blood from circulating? Not that I'd want you to do that, your subconscious won't allow it.

What about our youth? Can they stop themselves from growing or forming nerve or muscle tissue? Of course not. The physical power of the subconscious has an instinctive nature to preserve life, grow and heal.

Imagine if your subconscious had to think whether there was a right or wrong way for you to breathe or a right or wrong way for your heart to pump your blood. Your subconscious processes methodically and precisely without considering the possibility of whether it's doing it right or wrong.

The subconscious doesn't argue or even understand the difference between right and wrong or truth and fiction. It accepts everything as fact. Therefore, when you do something over and over, it becomes mechanical and is no longer an act of judgment by the conscious mind. It becomes a belief planted in your subconscious and is called upon instinctively without thought by your subconscious when needed.

This, of course, is awesome if the belief planted is empowering and consistent with your desires. However, it is harmful when the seed of thought is disempowering or based upon fear or any other painful emotion. It is essential to recognize the omnipotence of the subconscious mind and realize that this belief will be carried out regardless of whether it is pleasurable, painful, or even something you want.

How does the subconscious differ from the conscious mind? The conscious mind only deals with interpretations of the physical world through your five senses. It determines your beliefs associated with what you observe and has the power of reasoning. When you consider 'free will,' your conscious mind makes the choices for you.

Your conscious mind can direct your subconscious. The conscious mind interprets everything in the outer so that your subconscious can work like an efficient flawless machine relying upon the thoughts and beliefs planted by the conscious mind as fact. Our conscious mind protects our subconscious from all that is seen and observed while interpreting the information instead of taking it at face value.

For example, if you overhear a conversation that you completely disagree with, the fact that you consciously disagree is the truth planted in the subconscious mind. Your subconscious relies upon it as fact. Your conscious interpretation of the conversation gets buried in the subconscious mind. In this way, your conscious mind protects your subconscious from suggestions you disagree with and directs your subconscious actions to be consistent with your interpretations.

Remember that the subconscious mind never sleeps; it must be awake to keep the vital physical functions operating. Therefore, the conscious mind must protect the subconscious from outside influences. I once read about the concerns associated with your subconscious mind during surgery. General anesthesia knocks you out from a conscious perspective, but not from a subconscious perspective, as your vital organs continue to operate. Therefore, when you're influenced by general anesthesia, your subconscious is open to absorbing all that occurs without the filter of the conscious mind. Your conscious mind does not participate in shaping the suggestions made to the subconscious mind. Ultimately, when the conscious mind is not interpreting and shaping the recommendations to the subconscious mind, then the subconscious is left open to all the directions it experiences.

In summary, your conscious mind interprets through the five senses, then reasons, creating and shaping your beliefs. The subconscious mind operates instinctively upon those beliefs. The instincts in which the subconscious mind operates are shaped by the past reasoning of your subconscious mind.

Therefore, when your conscious mind interprets things and those interpretations are empowering, healthy, and constructive, your subconscious mind reaches accurate conclusions and is in harmony with Universal Energy, which is All-Powerful.

However, if your interpretations are disempowering, unhealthy, and destructive, your subconscious mind creates fear, worry, guilt, and many other destructive feelings and is not in harmony with Universal Energy. This is the cause of most mental and physical illnesses.

How do you eliminate disempowering, unhealthy, destructive beliefs? You suggest new empowering thoughts and feelings that will counteract the current beliefs. It can be as simple as stating specific, new, empowering suggestions or things you want to accomplish. The subconscious is naturally creative and connected to Universal Energy. The subconscious unites us with Omnipotence and will at once begin to work on your behalf with your new empowering thoughts and set the forces in an operation that will lead to the desired result. The more passion and feeling you can include in your new empowering suggestions, the more believable they will be and the more impact they will have. Your subconscious will accept the new thought as a new belief.

While you're having this conversation with yourself, in the back of your mind, you are thinking that the words you're saying are not valid, then understand, that is the belief you will develop.

Omnipotent Law is powerful. Those who have learned to master this law find harmony in situations and circumstances that others would expect to be complicated. Those who have learned to trust the power of the subconscious mind find that they have Infinite resources at their command – a direct connection to the Divine.

There is a difference between simply interpreting what comes our way and proactively directing our thoughts consciously, methodically, and constructively. When we proactively control our thoughts appropriately, we're in harmony with Universal Energy and begin to consciously be part of the creating process. The word 'constructively' is significant here. Universal Energy is harmonious. Destructive thoughts can never be in harmony with Universal Energy. This is what causes pain and illness, mental and physical. But when we direct our deliberate, empowering, constructive thoughts, we align with the harmony of Universal Energy and therefore align with the Divine. Natural law takes over.

Universal Energy is creative. It is the Creator. If the subconscious is united with Universal Energy, then it must be the same in form, nature, and quality as Universal Energy to some degree. Therefore, our subconscious mind is creative and will automatically correlate with its object of desire and bring it into manifestation. This law is called the *Law of Attraction*, which is how the subconscious mind will change circumstances or conditions on your behalf.

> *"We are not creatures of circumstances; we are creators of circumstance."*
>
> ~Benjamin Disraeli

Meditation Exercise Two

In meditation exercise one, you mastered securing control of the physical body. Now you're going to begin to control your thoughts.

Go to your room and get into position as reviewed in the Introduction. Be perfectly still as you were in Exercise One, then begin to hinder most thoughts. When you have a thought pop into your head, clear it immediately. This isn't easy if you are not used to controlling your thoughts.

One of the ways you can inhibit unwanted thoughts is to focus on your breathing. As you inhale, think about oxygen permeating every part of your body. As you exhale, count your exhales and envision all impurities leaving your body. As a new thought enters your mind, erase it and refocus on your breathing and oxygen permeating every part of your body and impurities exiting your body each time you exhale.

Counting your breath can also help hinder unwanted thoughts. Count to three as you inhale, and count to four as you exhale. Think about the air entering your lungs and negativity and impurities leaving your body as you exhale.

Being able to hinder thoughts will ultimately give you control over all thoughts and will enable you to direct your thoughts to only those you desire. Complete this exercise a minimum of six times until you can inhibit your thoughts and keep your thoughts directed to your breathing.

Before progressing to Chapter Three, you must master this exercise and understand this chapter strongly.

Our Bodies Are Miracles

Chapter Three

Like the relationship between the conscious and subconscious minds is the relationship between the corresponding nervous systems. The cerebrospinal system is the organ of the conscious mind, and the sympathetic nervous system is that of the subconscious mind.

The cerebrospinal system has its center in the brain and is the channel through which we consciously perceive or interpret through our five senses and control the movement of our bodies.

The sympathetic nervous system has its autonomous cluster of nerve cells at the back of the stomach and below the diaphragm, known as the celiac plexus or solar plexus. The solar plexus is the channel through which we subconsciously control most vital functions of our bodies, such as the lower part of the esophagus, pancreas, kidneys, liver, gallbladder, intestines, and stomach, for example.[7]

Mystics believe that the solar plexus chakra influences ego, intuition, personality, and your zest for life, among others, and directly reacts to your thoughts, which is how destructive, disempowering thoughts can directly affect your health. When your solar plexus is distressed, it can cause many health issues, such as heartburn, stomach pain, nausea, and acid reflux, to name a few milder symptoms. More severe impacts could result in the development of eating disorders, hypoglycemia, and even diabetes.[8]

Emotionally, it can result in feelings of helplessness, an excessive need for control, a victim mentality, and self-esteem and self-identity issues. [8]

Although science has recognized that negative emotions affect physical health,[9] it's about impossible to prove this to be true or untrue. However, anecdotal evidence supports this belief as it is evident that those that work solar plexus chakra healing practices are more mindful, intuitive, and physically healthy. Those that are angry, stressed, and full of anxiety have a weakened immune system which leads to more disease.[10]

Every thought is received by the brain and then subjected to your interpretation by the conscious mind. The conclusion of your interpretation becomes a belief or a truth for you, and that belief is planted in your subconscious mind. We have already learned that the subconscious doesn't reason or question things; it simply acts upon your truths and beliefs.

The solar plexus is considered the 'sun' of the body because it is the central point for energy to be distributed to the body. If the energy emitted from our sun is intense, then the individual is considered magnetic and charismatic. These individuals regularly influence others positively. You can feel their light and positive energy.

When the solar plexus emits intense energy, it radiates this vibrantly through the three dimensions of the subconscious: the physical, spiritual, and mental. The solar plexus provides the physical energy and vitality needed to sustain life. It radiates energy through the vagus nerve to the brain, which also provides us with spiritual energy. Everything in life is energy, and the solar plexus nerve energy, with its ability to operate independently of the brain, is truly remarkable.

Additionally, the solar plexus provides the mental energy the conscious mind needs. The conscious mind depends on the subconscious to support thought. Suppose the solar plexus is not emitting intense energy. In that case, the body isn't receiving what it needs to heal itself, the connection with the brain and Universal Energy is interrupted, and thoughts affect our mental health.

The solar plexus is where we, as finite beings, are united with the Infinite and where we, as eternal beings, are connected with Eternal Energy.

In summary, our conscious mind develops and stores our beliefs in the subconscious mind. In the second brain, our gut brain, the energy radiated from the solar plexus is vital to this process as it is the center of energy in which we are united with Universal Energy. The solar plexus radiates energy to everything in the body and beyond. The quality, character, and nature of our thoughts determine the quality, character, and nature of our energy being radiated. Therefore, our conscious mind develops what is emitted to the Universe. It is our conscious mind that influences Omnipotent Power.

Think about it for a moment... when you are one with Infinite Power, you can overcome any situation or circumstance by the power of your thoughts. When you consciously realize this power, you will have nothing to fear, and you can co-create your life with the Divine.

Exploring this in more depth is it's empowering, positive, non-resistant thought, that expands your solar plexus and produces intense energy to your body and subconscious mind. Disempowering, negative, resistant thoughts contract your solar plexus and drains the energy. All you must do is let your sunlight shine.

There are two categories of thoughts: one feels pleasurable, and the other feels painful. When your thoughts are pleasant, your inner sun shines and emits abundant energy. When your thoughts are negative and feel painful, clouds hide your sun, and your energy is drained with little left over for your body's health or mental clarity. What types of thoughts create a feeling of pain? Some fear generates every painful thought. This cannot be oversimplified, as it is fear that you must eliminate from your thoughts. Fear is your devil. Worry, guilt, criticism, etc., are all fearful feelings.

I received a message from an associate in which she attempted to explain why she didn't like her life right now. Below is a small portion of that message:

"…I may hate every second of it, but I always get through it… I just hate where I am right now, but it's the life I'm stuck in, so… you breathe through it and pretend and hope and pray the next life will be better… no-bid deal, it's always been this way."

This type of belief and self-talk will ensure that the future delivers the life you're 'stuck in,' and not only has it 'always been this way,' but it always will if this is the belief that has been planted into the subconscious mind as truth.

What you believe will determine your experience. If you are dissatisfied with your present situation in life, the only way to change it is to change your belief. If you expect nothing, you'll get nothing. If you expect greatness, you'll get greatness. The Omnipotent Power of the Divine is within you and will ultimately deliver precisely what you have faith in expecting.

Let's consider the question, "Whom do you say that I AM?" This isn't simply a question from Jesus to Peter. This is the question that everyone must answer themselves. In other words, 'Who do you say that you are?' Your conviction and belief in yourself will determine your expression in life. However, your answer to this question is precisely what determines your experience in life.

Your thoughts, which create your beliefs, are seen to be recognizing yourself to be what you expect for yourself. To consciously think of being poor and to hope for wealth will do nothing but deliver to you what you are conscious of being, which is lacking. 'Shutting the door' is shutting out what you are now aware of being and claiming yourself to be what you desire.

Instead of hoping for the desired result, you must expect it. Have faith and know it will be delivered. Know that wealth is your destiny and that your current circumstances are only a result of your past thoughts. Today, everything has changed. Today, it is only a matter of time before Omnipotent Power will deliver evidence of your wealth. The very moment that your desire becomes an expectation, the moment that it becomes what you know to be true for you and is a point of conviction, at that very moment, you begin to draw the evidence of your claim into your life.

"Faith is putting all your eggs in God's basket, then counting your blessings before they hatch."

~Ramona C. Carroll

Whatever the subconscious believes to be true is delivered to everyone and everything in the Universe as accurate, and the Infinite Power of the Universe provides evidence of that truth.

To apply this astonishing truth to your life, you must practice like anything else you have learned. It would be best if you first created empowering beliefs with your desires being the expected result. The most simple and effective way is to consciously concentrate on the object of your desire, not the lack thereof.

Identifying how you will produce the evidence of your newfound truth isn't necessary. As a finite being, with limitations of the conscious mind, you can't possibly determine the most creative solution. You must have faith in the Omnipotent Power of Universal Energy, which has unlimited resources and be open to the opportunities that will be presented.

Meditation Exercise Three

Now that you've mastered controlling your physical body and inhibiting thought, we will take it further. This time, you are to remain still, inhibit thought, and then add to your state by relaxing all the muscles and nerves in your body, releasing all tension.

Physical relaxation is a voluntary exercise of the conscious mind and enables the blood to circulate freely throughout the body and to and from the brain. Tension leads to abnormal mental activity, which some call restless mind syndrome.

If you find relaxing your body difficult, try to concentrate on feeling the pulse in your big toes one foot at a time. Once you feel it, stay focused on the pulse while you relax your feet. If a new thought pops into your mind, move to thoughts about your heels and again try to find and feel the pulse in your heels. Stay focused on the pulse and relax your body.

Again, move your thoughts to your knees if a new thought enters your mind. Concentrate on finding and feeling the pulse in your knees and relax your knees and legs. Continue this process on multiple body parts whenever a new thought enters your mind. You will find fewer interruptions of thought and an ability to release all tension in every part of your body.

Continue this until your body is completely relaxed, restful, and at peace with you and the world.

Relaxing every part of your body, and controlling your thoughts, is like rebooting a computer. The subconscious mind begins to operate from a fresh new perspective, and the solar plexus can resume working efficiently and instinctively.

The Spirit of the 'I' Within

Chapter Four

Many people contemplate who they are. You hear comments such as, 'I want to find myself.' Who is 'I' in this question? Is the 'I' your mind? Certainly not. The mind is like a computer that reasons and plans, but the mind doesn't have logic or the ability to think.

Is the 'I' your body? Although the 'I' tells your body what to do, it is something beyond.

What about your personality? The 'I' isn't your personality, either. Your core personality is developed over time based on all your life experiences, knowledge, and everything and everyone you have experienced since inception. However, the 'I' within you determines your likes and dislikes, which results in your personality.

When you say, 'I want' or 'I think,' the 'I' tells the mind what it wants or thinks. The 'I' instructs the body what to do and the 'I' determines your preferences, which create your personality.

"We are not human beings on a spiritual journey.
We are spiritual beings on a human journey."

~Stephen Covey

The 'I' is spiritual and the source of all power. When you say, 'I want to find myself.' You are saying that your Spirit, this 'I' within you and your inner voice, is not in alignment with the physical or outer world.

The most extraordinary power that your Spirit has is the power to think, and it is this power that shapes who you are and who you become.

Unfortunately, most of us haven't been taught how to think correctly, and therefore, we don't, which results in not attaining what we desire.

How do you think correctly? Every thought must consider all others in the Universe. Harm to anyone, including yourself, is not correct thinking. Every action or thought must benefit everyone involved and cannot be to anyone's detriment.

Many people think about acquiring things for selfish reasons. This is the germ that manifests negative results in your life. The more you think about serving others and realize that selfish thoughts are the poison that will kill any growth, the more you will come to know the true power of your thoughts.

You are part of the Universe. The 'I' within you is part of the Infinite. We are all connected, and as a part of the Infinite, we cannot provoke or alienate any other part of the Universe and benefit.

The happiness, peace, and harmony within the Universe depend upon each of us recognizing the interests of the Universe. So, everything affects everyone and everything in the Universe. Every action is felt throughout the Universe to some degree, yet you will never personally benefit from imposing harm on any part of the Universe.

This is one of the principles you must focus on to gain any form of happiness. The *Law of Reciprocity* – the Universe will deliver to you in an expanded proportion to what you provide to the Universe. With every thought if you keep this in mind, you will change your thoughts to be constructive and not waste time or money on things that don't work within this principle.

This becomes a habit through practice. Repetition is the mother of skill. If you aren't already a master of correct, constructive thinking, now is the time to teach yourself. *The Law of Fair Exchange* says that your result will be directly proportional to your effort. Therefore, you will benefit from learning and integrating this principle directly to the effort you extend in learning it right now.

Here's where you can start.

- I can be what I decide to be.
- I can be what I will myself to be.
- I can be what I desire to be.

Begin repeating these vision statements every morning, every night, and multiple times throughout the day until they become beliefs while keeping in mind who and what the 'I' really is. The spiritual 'I' understands you cannot gain by harming any other within the Universe.

Eventually, through repetition, this practice creates a new habit. Habits are formed by repeatedly doing or saying something until your subconscious has accepted it as a belief you instinctively act upon.

You will begin to believe these statements, and you will instinctively act upon this belief. When you instinctively act upon these statements of belief, and they are impregnated with love for everyone, you will become invincible.

Right now, try to pick up an object near you. Were you able to pick it up? Of course, you were. Trying is doing. Anything you try to do, you do. If you don't do it, it's because you didn't try; you decided not to do it. You either picked up the object or didn't; whichever you did was your choice. That choice begins to create habits that empower you or disempower you.

Don't try to do anything. To quote Nike, '*Just Do It*' or don't do it, but don't say you'll try when you know you have no intentions of following through. This creates a habit of failure, one of the most disempowering habits you can make.

Below is the cycle of creating a new habit...

- Unconscious incompetence: We don't know what we don't know
- Conscious incompetence: We realize what we don't know.
- Conscious competence: If we consciously think about it, we can do it right.
- Unconscious competency: We don't have to give it much thought, and we can still do it correctly.

The unconscious competency stage is when a new thought has become a habit and becomes automatic. The subconscious mind considers it valid, and there is no longer any doubt about it.

For example, since this information is likely new to you, you may be at the conscious incompetence stage when it comes to thinking correctly. Practice, and perfect repetition, will progress your thinking to a conscious competency, and in due time, you will have created the habit of thinking correctly.

Let's relate this to habits of failure. Have you created a habit of failure? Instead of living your life based on the habit of failure, you can live your life based on the habit of success, which is a requirement for abundant living. What's the success habit? It is simple... do what you say you will do. Starting something with no intention of finishing creates a pattern of failure. Think about it. If you set achievable goals and don't follow through three out of four times, you have created a belief that you fail seventy-five percent of the time at whatever you decide to accomplish. This is highly disempowering.

Jim Rohn, a business philosopher I respect immensely, says, "*Something easy to do is also easy not to do.*" Don't get into the habit of not completing your easy predetermined goals. You create the habit of failure instead of the habit of success.

When you decide, you must follow through because the lack of following through creates the habit of failure. If this has been your past, change it today. Decide that you will repeat these vision statements morning, night, and several times throughout the day. You may want to commit to doing this for only two weeks. Then after you've been successful, extend it two more weeks, and so on.

Once you have committed yourself, you will have planted a seed of an empowering belief about your ability to be what you desire at will. You will also have planted a seed that can grow into a habit so deep within your subconscious that when your goal is more significant, your subconscious will kick in and execute based on your new habit of success.

Ultimately, do not say you'll 'try' to do something that you are capable of doing unless you are committed to following it through.

When you learn to do what you say you're going to do, not only will you gain credibility with everyone you encounter, but you will find the power within that controls your outer world; your reality, the power within that ultimately delivers to you in the outer world the evidence of your beliefs.

If you think about it, this isn't that surprising to consider. You are part of the Infinite, in which we are all united. Scientifically, nothing is more certain than that we are in the presence of an Infinite and Eternal Energy to which we are all connected.

Most religions consider God as being within us, as well. The Bible says, *"Know ye not that ye are the temple of God, and that the Spirit of God dwelleth in you?"* There are many times in the Bible that this is stated over and over again. *'I AM the Shepherd,' 'I and my Father are One.'* And so on...

Here is the SECRET OF MASTERY: The Infinite is within you, is All-Powerful, has unlimited resources, and has everything in abundance. With this power, you can accomplish anything you desire that respects all parts of the Universe.

The first requirement of being of service to others is having the means to do so. You cannot be generous to others unless you have abundance. You cannot give and serve others unless you are strong. The Spirit within you has the right to the abundance in the Universe to be strong to help others. The Spirit within has access to all the abundance, and as long as you live within the *Law of Reciprocity* and the *Law of Love*, what you desire is within your command.

The Infinite expresses and creates through the individual, and the individual expresses through the Universe. When you're in alignment with all that is good and being of service to the Universe, the Spirit within you sets the forces in motion so that the Infinite can create through you. Seek inspiration and connect with your Spirit within.

Your Spirit within can deliver you your heart's desire. It is creative, and it is what brings you to life. Without Spirit, you are nothing. If your Spirit were to die or leave your body, you would cease to exist. Your Spirit will assist you in attracting abundance and will work to deliver to you the evidence of your beliefs. Your realization and acknowledgment that God is within you will allow you access to life's abundance.

If you recall, the cause behind all effects is within. Your Spirit is the part of you that is part of the Infinite. It is the part that is the Creator within your conscious influence. You must realize your conscious power due to your unity with this All-Powerful Spirit.

Your conscious thoughts create your habits and beliefs. They make your awareness of who you are or your awareness of being. So, it is crucial for you to understand your conscious power.

Seek silence and stillness often because if you quiet your mind and body, you can think correctly. It is thought that is the secret to creativity and, ultimately, your ability to manifest your desires.

The *Law of Vibration* carries light and electricity. We know it works even though we don't see it. Thought, similarly, is carried through the *Law of Vibration*. So thought vibrates beyond our physical being and is united with the Infinite.

Now consider the *Law of Love*. Love is directly aligned with the Infinite, so thoughts based on Love are given vitality.

The last law in this process is the *Law of Growth*. It's the law in which thoughts take form and expression. Emotions give feeling to thoughts so that thoughts will take shape. If you have a thought based upon the *Law of Love*, that thought is in direct alignment and united with the Infinite and takes form through the *Law of Growth*.

How do you develop the faith, courage, and passion for accomplishing this chain of events that will ultimately express your thoughts and desires to you? It's simple: practice and repetition.

Meditation Exercise Four

In this exercise, you'll mentally relax and let go of all stress and all negative feelings and thoughts. As always, do not progress to this exercise if you haven't mastered the ability to physically relax in Exercise Three.

Think of your computer, which has multiple processes running and gets locked up because there's so much going on that its memory can't handle it. So, you reboot your computer, and it begins to work again the way it was meant to work. That is what we're doing here. Your solar plexus needs to be radiating energy to every part of the body. Your conscious mind relies upon a radiating solar plexus for instinctive thought. When you reboot your system, your body and mind begin to process correctly again.

Take your normal position, still and relax your body. Take as much time necessary to relax the body and remain still. Simultaneously, inhibit outside thoughts, and then remove all tension in your mind.

Let go of all adverse conditions, such as hatred, anger, worry, jealousy, envy, sorrow, trouble, or disappointment. This may be difficult, but you cannot let your emotions control you right now; you must allow your intellect to take over and control your emotions. Release all negativities. You can let go of these things. Once you do, you will experience mental freedom.

The quality of your thought correlates to its object in your outer world. Your ability to consciously release all disempowering thoughts will lead to mental freedom and is the first step in allowing you to consciously direct your use of the universal *Law of Attraction* from which there is no escape.

As a reminder, you want to do this for no less than ten minutes daily. However, begin to lengthen the time to twenty minutes daily. Continue this exercise until you can quickly and easily get yourself in this state. Once you have mastered this, you will no longer be enslaved to your body and mind, and you are well on your way to your body and mind becoming enslaved to you.

The Conscious Choice of Your Heredity

Chapter Five

You have heard that most of us use only about ten percent of our mental power. That's because more than ninety percent of our mental power is subconscious, and most of us use only a tiny portion of our subconscious as we rely upon our conscious mind for most of our power. Yet the subconscious can solve anything and everything. So how do we tap into this power?

Let's first understand how you have come to be the person you have become. You recognize that your subconscious mind manages every part of your physical body and that your objective or conscious mind can influence your subconscious by creating new beliefs and expectations through your thoughts.

Heredity is the predominant source behind the mind that permeates the body. Heredity gives us our attitude, organ function, control over movement, blood circulation, nerve and muscle strength, bone structure, and many other physical things. Mentally, we are the total of everything and everyone we have experienced, including what has been passed onto us through all past generations. This is important to understand because it can play a massive role in the person you become.

Most of us accept our heredity without question, and that acceptance becomes who we are because we believe it is who we are. On the other hand, if you think that you will be different because what you expect of yourself and what you know you can become is unlike that of your past generations, then that is what you will become. You have a choice as to which of the inherited characteristics you embrace and which you do not. Those that are desirable, you should consciously use. For those that are undesirable, you need to get rid of them deliberately.

Today, you are the result of your past thinking, regardless of what you inherited, and you will become what you are thinking about today in the future. The *Law of Attraction* will bring what you think about, not what you desire, wish, or hope for, but what you focus on and have created in your mind's eye by your thoughts.

If the thoughts that consume your mind are of fear, doubt, negativity, apprehension, worry, guilt, etc., this will be the result of what enters your life. If the thoughts that enter your mind are happy, optimistic, positive, excited, abundant, enthusiastic, faithful, courageous, healthy, etc., that will be the result of what enters your life.

Ultimately, the quality of the thoughts you generate comes back to you and will be evident in the circumstances in your life, similar to a gravitational pull that attracts like.

The best physical scientists cannot account for initial creation or the origination of life, not through heredity or evolution. This Infinite Life flows through you, the power that comes from the 'I' within you that flows directly from the Infinite or Universal Energy in which we are all united.

You inherit your physical traits from your parents and all past generations. You inherit the power within you from the Infinite or Universal Energy in which you are in the image and likeness. Understand that this inheritance gives you power over weakness, fear, negativity, and intimidation.

This Infinite Power within you is active with use. You are the vessel in which the Infinite Power is differentiated into physical form. We've mentioned before that the Universe creates through the individual. Therefore, unless you give and allow the Infinite Power to create through you, the vessel is blocked, and you cannot receive its power. Use is a condition associated with inheriting this power. The more we give, the more we get. Remember the *Law of Reciprocity* and the *Law of Love*. The Universe will return to you in a multiplied proportion to what you give.

Complete a 'mental house-cleaning' every day. Mental, moral, and physical purity is essential to mastering empowering expectations and ultimately empowering realities. This is as simple as the choices you make. Suppose you choose to eliminate negative thoughts, refuse to have anything to do with them, and redirect your thoughts to those that are positive and empowering. In that case, that choice will deliver in your physical world situations and circumstances worthy of your thoughts.

You can have complete power over the circumstances that arise in your physical world by claiming in your thoughts the environment in which you insist upon living. You must not only have a desire but also claim it as yours and own it throughout your thoughts. Become it in consciousness. Health, harmony, and abundance are just a few rewards; the only requirement is the commitment to practice the skills that make the 'right' thinking a habit.

To attain more loving relationships, you must become more loving to others. You must be more abundant in what you do to attain more abundance. To achieve financial freedom, you must become free from financial burdens. All power is contingent upon adequately using the power already in your possession. Use this Infinite Power within you for the good of all, and you will become more powerful and not only give others more but simultaneously begin living an abundant life.

Meditation Exercise Five

For every meditation exercise, beginning with this exercise through the final meditation exercise, you are to start as follows:

- Still the body
- Still the mind
- Relax the body
- Relax (release) the mind

The next step is to visualize. The balance of the exercises will ask you to imagine a perfect picture. Before progressing to visualization, you must complete stilling and relaxing the body and mind.

Additionally, it is crucial to visualize the result desired, not how you get there or the lack thereof. If you envision your health, see yourself as vibrant and cured; if you want financial wealth, see yourself in your new home.

Some will consider meditation and visualization as prayer. If you are praying for another, see that person in the situation that you desire them to be in. For example, if you are praying for someone ill, in your mind's eye, envision the favorable desirable situation and give thanks for their healing.

In this meditation, you will transition from stilling and relaxing the mind and body to visualizing a pleasant situation. Make a complete mental picture of it. See the buildings, grounds, trees, friends, associations, and everything complete.

At first, you will probably think of everything under the sun except the ideal upon which you desire to concentrate. That's okay, but eventually, you want to picture your desired situation. Practice this meditation exercise every day without fail until you have it mastered. Continue to visualize the same desired result.

Our Thoughts Are Energy in Motion

Chapter Six

Universal Energy not only has unlimited resources but can produce unlimited results and has Infinite Intelligence.

"I am in perfect harmony with the working of the law. I stand aside and let Infinite Intelligence make easy and successful my way."

~Florence Scovel Shinn

Universal Energy can produce any result at any time for anyone. So how do we use this Infinite Power to make the desired results or circumstances?

Let's consider the effects of electricity as a parallel to understand the effects of Universal Energy better. The Universe today doesn't have any more electricity within its realm than it did in the 1800s. Yet today we have digital audio players, heat pumps, and power to our homes and businesses. The effects of electricity today are significantly improved over what most couldn't even imagine in the 1800s, and one hundred years from now, the effects of electricity will probably be much more significant.

Electricity is a form of energy in motion, and its effects depend upon the electrical device connected to this form of energy. This motion of energy through the attached device can create music, heat, cool air, light, and many other things depending upon the device. But without the audio player, electricity doesn't produce music; without electricity, the audio player doesn't make music. Without a compatible device and the proper wiring, electricity can't possibly produce a thing.

But as we learn and expand our understanding of the wiring and how we make things work with electricity, we create more opportunities for its use.

What is the effect of Universal Energy? Like electricity, Universal Energy, in which we are all connected, cannot produce anything independently. It requires thought. The Universe today doesn't have any more ability to create effects through thought than it did in the 1800s or will one hundred years from now. However, as we learn and expand our understanding and power of this Universal Energy, we create more opportunities through thought.

Thought is a form of energy in motion, like electricity or cellular service and its effect depends upon the device or mind with which the thought is connected. This energy in motion through the mind of an individual can create anything. The creations or effects produced are the result of the action and reaction of the individual upon the Universe through thought. The human brain makes all of this happen. The human brain is the thought device in which thoughts take form.

Every thought sets the brain cells in motion. However, concentrated thought sets the forces in motion to express your thought perfectly in form. Concentrated thought can cause the elimination of any undesirable circumstance and the attainment of any desirable occasion. Focused thought is the essential factor associated with the power within you. It is what will allow you to accomplish anything at will.

Concentrated thought is how you consciously visualize your desired result and hold it in your mind until it is planted into your subconscious and becomes part of who you are. Once you ascend in consciousness to whom you desire to be, and your desired result is part of who you are, you have the Spirit of Power that connects you with Universal Truth.

This sounds simple. Not necessarily. However, it can be learned. Try focusing on a single purpose for ten minutes. You may find that your mind roams, and you'll need to bring it back into focus. This roaming usually doesn't create the concentrated thought required to bring your thought into reality. Invest some time in the greatest invention ever, the human brain, and practice. Repetition is the mother of skill.

Fortunately, with practice, you will improve your ability in this regard significantly. Once you have mastered concentrating your thoughts on a single definite purpose in harmony with the Divine, the results will be excellent.

In the original *Master Key*, Charles Haanel compared the power of thought to that of a magnifying glass. If you focus it long enough with the sun's energy appropriately aligned, it is incredible what the magnifying glass can accomplish. Similarly, concentrated thought on a definite purpose aligned with our sun or in harmony with the Divine can produce results that are just amazing.

There is a tremendous mental world in which we live; it is united with Universal Energy, and it is All-Powerful. Our mental world will respond to our thoughts proportionate to our faith and purpose. The more the goal is in harmony with the Universe, meaning all that is good and constructive, without destruction to any part of the Universe, and the greater our faith and passion, the greater the strength to manifest.

Learn to remove yourself from the many activities and thoughts of your day-to-day life to have time for reflection and directive thinking. These are essential to generate a constructive mental attitude. You develop discernment and a more precise understanding and appreciation of facts. If you look within and focus on the universal laws that consistently deliver a predetermined result, you will eventually come into vibrational alignment with what is most desirable in life.

The most extraordinary ideas come to those who are receptive and open themselves up to receive. When you're in harmony with Universal Energy, you are united with everyone and everything in the Universe; with this harmony, you master the principles of thinking and connecting with Omnipotent Power.

In this harmonious state, your thoughts expand universally, and you will find that your environment and circumstances follow your mental and spiritual development. Begin by identifying the Spirit within you, and then the opportunity will be made available to you through perception, knowledge, and inspired thought. Knowledge sparks growth, and inspired thought will prompt action, which results in a transformation into Infinite and unlimited possibilities.

Meditation Exercise Six

This exercise begins to work on visualization techniques. Get a photograph or use an image of someone you love immensely in your life on your phone or tablet. Bring it to your room, get into position, and study the photograph carefully. Note each feature, eye color, shape, feeling, and even any birth marks, freckles or lines on their face. Now close your eyes and meditate as you learned in meditation exercises one through four.

Once you're in a meditative state with your muscles, nerves, and mind relaxed, try to see that someone you love in your mind's eye. See your loved one mentally in the same level of detail. Are you able to picture them perfectly? If you can, that's awesome! You are well on your way to using the power of visualization.

If you're not there yet, repeat this until you can create the picture in your mind's eye that significantly resembles the photograph.

This exercise will prepare your mind for a new habit that you will work on creating. Visualization is one of the primary techniques you will use to control or direct your thoughts and is the primary tool used when concentrating on a definite purpose that you desire to manifest.

Dream Perfect Dreams

Chapter Seven

Your imagination is potent and the primary process you'll use to design your future. Whatever picture you can vividly imagine in your mind's eye can become your reality. Can you dream? Can you imagine and create without limitation? If you can, you can attract it into your life.

Like planning a successful business, you must plan for a successful life. Therefore, the first step in the planning process is to decide. You must decide what you want. Effective visualization or the idealization of the perfect plan will be your guide in that process.

This could be the most challenging step for some, but it is essential. Meditation is needed to give you the clarity of thinking you'll need and is the method by which concentrated thought becomes powerful. There are no limitations except for those you have placed upon yourself. Your power to think is unlimited; therefore, through Universal Energy, your power to create your reality is also unlimited, so throw out all preconceived notions of what can and cannot be. There are no limitations in your imagination.

Your goal is to define the desired result clearly. Don't get attached to the means, just the result. Now hold that image in your mind and do it daily. You must commit to visualization daily. This commitment will generate the concentration and focus that will deliver your dreams to reality.

Concentrating thoughts on a definite purpose will unknowingly set the forces in motion to deliver the evidence of your being. A general picture may be where you start. Then the details will gradually unfold and take shape until progressively, you hold a clear view of your result, which will eventually materialize in your physical world.

If you have difficulties creating your perfect picture in your mind, make it using today's technology in a slide show or movie and then continue to watch the movie, this will spark the fire that will allow you to see the light, which will deliver a clear mental picture for your imagination to expand upon.

A movie isn't the answer. However, the images in your mind, including you in the picture, will influence your subconscious mind to accept it as truth. Think about the Universe and all its abundance for a moment. Could the Universe be created by accident? No, not likely.

Now consider the higher power behind this incredible creation that ultimately created the Universe and that we are united with the same Universal Mind as that of the creator. That same Universal Mind created the Universe operating through the individual or you and gives you the power to create your reality.

Anything created today is being created through the individual. Any new product, service, or invention is first imagined in the mind of its creator. And a great athlete or performer imagines their perfect performance before it comes to fruition. Any great architect conceives the structure they intend to build before it is put to paper and in its final form. And all of these cases, the picture of the desired result must first be vivid in thought before it ever can be reality.

Similarly, you must have a clear, vivid picture of the desired result as you wish it to be. Savor the feeling of enjoying your life this way. Imagine that you have already achieved it and are now living it. You must ascend in consciousness and become whom you desire to be.

Not only does imagining things from this perspective allow you to understand what will become of your future, but you will also develop faith, confidence, endurance, courage, and enthusiasm for your desires. You will develop a passion for your desires and life.

Begin to dream perfect dreams. Don't worry about the current reality. Imagine a beautiful, abundant world with peace and happiness, where everything goes your way, and begin to be the person in your perfect dream. The Universe will correspond to your command. Life will be rearranged and become what you have imagined for you.

"All breaks you need in life wait within your imagination. Imagination is the workshop of your mind, capable of turning mind energy into accomplishment and wealth."

~Napoleon Hill

Visualize the perfect image and hold it in your mind. Feel the way it feels. The rest will unfold, and you will be led to your desires. You will be given opportunities to expand and develop into what you desire. You will be inspired to take a path at the right time to achieve the desired effect.

Why have we been taught to look to our outer world for strength? We have been taught that it is the things we do that give us power and results. This is not the truth. It's not some supernatural power that only the fortunate few are blessed with; everyone has this ability.

You have millions of brain cells and billions of competent cells in your body. Each of these cells has the intelligence to act upon any suggestion, and they have the psychic ability to attract whatever is necessary to carry out any suggestion. They do this through the *Law of Attraction* and silently attract what they need to survive. They take your suggestions as truth and attract what they need to accomplish your vision.

You know people who want money, power, health, and abundance but never seem to realize it. The issue in most cases is that they are trying to attain what they desire by doing something in the outer world without focusing upon their inner world. They think that they can achieve what they want by changing something in the outer world instead of changing who they are in their inner world. They need to realize how to bring the *Law of Attraction* into action. They never seek answers from their Spirit that can dream perfect dreams and has unlimited resources. They don't understand that looking for wisdom, peace, and truth from within is the key to setting the *Law of Attraction* into operation.

Wisdom will open the source of power that will manifest in thought and purpose, creating your desired reality.

If you imagine debt and continually think about it, concentrating on it over and over, worried about it, not only will your situation not improve, but it will also lead to more outstanding debt. Through the *Law of Attraction*, concentrating on debt brings about more debt.

If you imagine wealth and continually think about it, concentrating on it over and over, making decisions with the wisdom of the wealthy, and being excited about it, you guessed it. Your situation will improve. It will lead to wealth. Through the *Law of Attraction*, concentrating on wealth brings about more wealth.

Think about this for a moment: have you ever met a person who believes, 'I can't ever get a break?' That person's right, aren't they? What about the clumsy person who says, 'I'm so clumsy.' That person is regularly clumsy, aren't they?

On the other hand, do you know anyone who believes everything always seems to go right for them? That person is usually right as well.

"If you think you can, or if you think you cannot, you are always right."

~Henry Ford

So why is it so challenging to think about what you desire as if you already have it versus thinking about the desire as something that you are lacking? Many tend to be too anxious and have anxiety, fear, or worry about things.

You must make the investment and stay focused on what's desired through meditation and visualization, and then allow the investment to grow. You must practice. Create the picture, dream the dream, throw away any preconceived notions of limitations, and be who it is you desire to be in consciousness. This does not mean doing nothing. You must act upon inspired thought that leads you toward your desires. Opportunities will be delivered to you, and you will have become the person you desire to be in consciousness. Then as the opportunities arise, you will instinctively act upon them.

Ask yourself this, and then be patient and reflect upon your thoughts and beliefs. 'Do you now and then feel the Spirit within you?' Does the spiritual 'I' within you determine your direction, or do you follow the crowd? Please don't allow the negativity of others, and their preconceived limited beliefs, to become your thoughts and, therefore, your reality. You can do anything you will yourself to be!

Exercise Meditation Seven

In meditation exercise 6, you began visualization techniques. You were asked to get a photograph of someone in your life whom you love and to visualize this photo in every detail. Can you picture the image in your mind's eye? If you can, then feel free to progress. Otherwise, continue with exercise 6 until you have mastered it.

Now take your position, and with this same image, visualize your loved one. See this person as you saw them last. Recall the conversation you had and imagine the person's face. See it distinctively. Now talk to your loved one about a mutual interest. See the expression on their face and how it changes. Here your loved one talk and watch them smile. Can you do this?

If you can, spark their interest by telling them a story about an adventure or trip. Talk to your loved one about something you want to do with them as if you had already been there and you're now sharing your experience with them. See your loved one's face light up with this spirit of fun or excitement. Feel their excitement. Feel your passion.

Can you do all of this? If not, with practice, you will get there. Once you can do this, you will consciously improve your imagination, which is exceptional progress toward mastering the *Law of Attraction*.

The Basic Instinct of Love

Chapter Eight

Although many consider our basic instinct one of survival, we are ensured survival. We are eternal beings, so survival is imminent. Our basic instinct is one of love. This instinct has us protecting others and feeling sad when others are harmed. The *Law of Love*: love everything and everyone in the Universe, respect, love, light, truth, and peace. These are the virtues of natural law. The more you align with the *Law of Love*, the more power you will realize to create your future reality.

Notice that it is quite impossible for you to be filled with love, respect, light, truth, and peace and be negative and have destructive thoughts. The natural *Law of Love* makes positive thoughts much more powerful than negative thoughts. It's how we were meant to be. It's what we instinctively are. The law also prevents those who strive for abundance yet never consider benefits to others from ever achieving abundance. This selfishness may attract money, but it doesn't attract abundance.

We are to hate nothing – NOTHING! Not even what is perceived as bad because hatred is highly destructive, and destructive thoughts and beliefs will result in a future reality of destruction.

Have you ever seen great things come to those who are negative and think of lack and conformity regularly? No. The most significant results come from the most positive, creative people. You cannot get a healthy positive environment for yourself if your thoughts are predominantly negative, just as you cannot get an unhealthy negative environment if your thoughts are always positive and consistent with the greater good of all.

We have two general categories of emotions, those that feel good and those that feel bad. There's nothing in the natural *Law of Love* that should feel bad. When you feel good, you're working in alignment with the *Law of Love*. When you feel bad, you are not in alignment with the *Law of Love*. These feelings that feel bad are emotions based upon fear. When we have emotions that don't feel good, this is the spirit within us telling us we're off track and that we need to get back on track. Feelings that don't feel good are not meant to make our lives miserable. They're just meant to give us the feedback we need to change our course. We're not supposed to embrace bad feelings and allow them to linger.

Thoughts are the creative principle of the Universe and combine with other similar thoughts. The *Law of Growth* says that everything instinctively will grow. So negative thoughts will tend to grow more hostile, and positive thoughts will have a strong tendency to grow more pleasurable. Because the *Law of Love* is as strong as it is and our natural state of being, positive thoughts and positive things based on love grow much faster than negative thoughts and things. In either case, the *Law of Growth* will take thoughts into form and bring them into our reality.

The *Law of Attraction* always works this way, and your future reality depends upon your predominant mental attitude and habits, the words you say to yourself, and the pictures you've created in your mind.

> *"The most important words you will ever hear are the words you say to yourself. So, make them positive. Make them kind."*
>
> ~Marissa Peer

If you're thinking about lack and have negative thoughts all day, and then you decide to meditate for 20 minutes with positive thoughts, this will not likely bring you positive results because your predominant mental attitude and habits are negative. Your dominant mental attitude and habits must change, not just those you force yourself to have now and then but your everyday, all-the-time thoughts. Remember that the *most important words you'll hear are the words that you say to yourself* in thought.

Any thought that we persist in cannot fail to manifest. So thoughts of fear bring more fear. Thoughts of love for others bring you love. Thoughts that include hate of others bring you hate. Thoughts of abundance bring you abundance.

Thoughts of joy bring you joy. Thoughts of financial wealth bring you financial wealth.

Creating habits that naturally allow your thoughts to bring you what you desire is a tremendous investment. Additionally, since our natural state of being is instinctively in love, the thoughts that are positive and beneficial to all thrive.

You must see your negative feelings just as they were meant to be, as the negative feedback you need to know you are off track and to prompt you to change course. When you have a fearful or negative thought, your objective is to understand what is causing it. You can correct or change your thoughts to those that are more constructive. You must quickly and efficiently get rid of the negative thoughts. One way to eliminate a disempowering negative thought is to release it consciously.

Anytime a disempowering thought enters your mind, you eliminate it. You take a deep breath and release the negative. Focus on clearing your mind, just as taught in the meditation exercises.

The second method is to replace the disempowering negative thought with one that is positive and empowering. Most people find substituting another thought easier than eliminating a thought with no substitute. In other words, if you fill your mind with enough empowering thoughts, there won't be enough room to focus on the disempowering thought. Since the conscious mind has limited capabilities, unlike the subconscious, this method works and is a bit easier to manage.

Your imagination can do wonders for you in this regard. Close your eyes and imagine everything around you precisely the way you desire. Can you do this in your mind's eye? If you can, this is how you substitute your thoughts. You imagine it the way you desire.

The first step in mastering the *Law of Attraction* is recognizing that the real power comes from your inner voice or the spirit within you. You must realize your oneness with everyone in the Universe, your unity with the All-Powerful. Through your unity with the Universal Energy, your mind is the only creative principle within your control that is All-Powerful. Your creative thought, or imagination, ultimately takes form when in harmony with the natural *Law of Love* or all that is good. Until this realization occurs, you likely are trying to physically change your outer world versus changing it from the spirit within you that is united with everyone and everything and respects and loves all. The power we seek is spiritual, and it is what lies in the hearts of all things. It is the soul of the Universe.

The next step is to tap into this spiritual power, which will require you to think and act in a manner that allows you to receive this power, which ultimately means, practice, drill, and rehearse.

If you're not growing, you are dying. Thought is the origin of your growth and what prompts your conscious evolution. Everything you can create will first be created in your mind and later manifested into a reality.

Daydreaming is a form of mental dissipation, so don't mistake daydreaming for a form of imagination. Imagination is a form of creation. Imagination can create in your mind the perfect reality you desire. Using your imagination, unlike daydreaming, takes practice.

You must hold mental ideals of what you desire, and as you begin to attract bits and pieces of what you need to manifest your ideal, you constantly maintain in your mind's eye the desired result. Upon holding a mental ideal or perfect picture of what you desire, when opportunities present, you'll recognize them, receive them, and ultimately manifest the reality in direct proportion to your commitment to your perfect picture.

Imagination is the process that begins creating your heaven on earth. The power of imagination is how you can build a strong foundation of spiritual energy to support the vertical construction of your future. You can be protected from harm and live in abundance in all aspects of your life for eternity.

Meditation Exercise Eight

This week we'll take an object back to its origination. Use your analytical skills and look below the surface for its cause. Go as far back as possible and determine what prompted the physical object or activity.

Take your position and visualize something pleasurable. It could be your current home, the career you love, or anything that is pleasurable to you. Visualize this pleasantry in your mind's eye. Now go back to when you first saw your home or started the job you love.

- How did you come upon this thing, activity, or person?
- How did the object get there?
- How did the activity originate?
- How did you meet the person?
- When was it built?

Could you bring it back even further? In the case of an activity, when did it originate, and how? When was it designed, who designed it, and what were they thinking? If you're thinking about a relationship, how did you meet the person, and why is it that this person fits the bill? Even earlier, what materials are in the home? Is it a concrete foundation? Is it steel-reinforced? What about the change in construction styles? What influenced the styles? You get the idea. Take this so far back and visualize every step until you can't take it back any further.

It is probable that your home, career, or relationship originated with yourself or if taken back even further, by original thought. Regardless of what you choose, it originated as an individual thought, a group of people with a consensus of thought, or the creator's original thought. Isn't that correct? We likely find in the last analysis that our own thought or thoughts of society is responsible for this pleasurable experience and many other things seldom thought of.

You'll find exercises of this kind invaluable. Everything appears differently when the thought has been trained to look below the surface. The insignificant becomes significant, and the uninteresting becomes interesting. The things that were supposed to be unimportant are seen as the only vital things in existence.

The Perfect Spirit Within

Chapter 9

Most of our desires are focused on health, wealth, and love. The order of importance may vary, but most likely, all our desires fit within one of these categories. Love certainly is something that most can't live without, and that is love that gives us what we need to have fulfillment in all categories.

Without the love of self, it is quite challenging to prioritize your health. It is also difficult for others to trust you if you don't inherently show love for others, and trust is a crucial trait you must have to attract relationships that will lead to wealth.

In any regard, most will agree that fulfilling your health, wealth, and love desires will result in a joyous, abundant life. Learning to think correctly is how such a life can be delivered.

How do you think correctly? It's pretty simple. Your thinking must be consistent with truth. Think about it. If it's true, it's inevitable. The truth shall set us free, correct?

Most can predict an outcome when they know the result will be based on a universal truth, wouldn't you agree? Is the sun going to rise tomorrow? Of course, it is. Would you believe it if I told you that tomorrow would be different? Tomorrow the moon will rise instead of the sun. Would you believe me? Of course not.

You can't believe it because you know it's not true. Therefore, relying upon a result when the basis of the action is not true will result in an unexpected or undesirable outcome, and therefore we should avoid it.

What is true as it relates to the ideal state of being? What do you think as spiritual beings our true actual natural state of being is likely to be? Is it probable that our natural state of being is in harmony with the Divine? If you learn the truth about your natural state of being, you can have faith that anything you desire can be attained.

Let's explore the core universal truth of our higher power, which most consider perfect, strong, powerful, loving, and harmonious. Our higher power, the Infinite, the Universal Mind, God, Eternal Energy, the Divine, or whatever you call the Almighty, and which we are all united, is no less than perfect and within each of us. We are all one in spirit.

Whatever characteristics are possessed by our higher power, therefore, are also within each of us, within our Spirit. Spiritually we are perfect, strong, powerful, loving, and harmonious.

Thought is a creative spiritual activity. If you hold a thought in your mind, the perfect Spirit within you must deliver conditions and harmony with your thought. Thought is spiritual, and the Spirit is perfect and powerful. Therefore, thought must be in harmony with the circumstances delivered to you in the outer world.

If you desire financial wealth, understand that your Spirit is perfect and powerful and must deliver an outer world that is in harmony with your inner world. Therefore, you change your thoughts and concentrate on financial wealth for you and all. The perfect, powerful Spirit within will bring you into vibration with the forces that will deliver to you the circumstances that match your thoughts and manifest financial wealth. This is the 'truth' about the All-Powerful Spirit within you.

Your imagination is the key to your spiritual power. Your imagination is the creative expression of your inner world. Seeing things in your mind's eye is very different from seeing things with your eyes. Your eyes see things only in your outer world, and the outer world is only the result of your inner world. Your inner world is the cause or action that creates the outer world. Creative visualization in your mind's eye allows your powerful Spirit to set the spiritual forces in motion that bring you into vibration with what you focus on giving you the result in your outer world.

Your greatest spiritual truth is that you're perfect, strong, loving, and harmonious Spirit is united with the Infinite and always brings you into vibration with what you focus on. It is guaranteed.

Many medical miracles have been documented that show the power of thought. Thought can change the result associated with what most would consider incurable. How does this happen? Time and time again, it is explained by faith. The individual believes so strongly in the Infinite Power that they will change the outcome simply by willing it to be.

The Infinite is All-Powerful and can eliminate all fear, lack, and pain and attract all pleasure, abundance, and joy.

Time and time again, those who have been fortunate to have this faith cure their supposedly incurable disease by creating a vision and affirmations focusing upon what is most needed, claiming it repeatedly.

This behavior is a choice that can be learned and applied to any situation you desire. You are to create a vision statement opposite to the current undesirable situation. Substitute the disempowering thought with the empowering thought for you and all and think it repeatedly.

Whenever you send out thoughts that are good for all, they return multiplied. For example, 'I am perfect, strong, powerful, loving, and harmonious' can easily be said, 'we are all perfect, strong, powerful, loving, and harmonious.' Rotating these two vision statements is oh-so powerful.

Now how are you going to ensure that you think only empowering thoughts? You must eliminate negative, disempowering thoughts as they enter your mind. This is easier said than done. At first, you'll find that disempowering thoughts pop into your head regularly. You must forget... eliminate... terminate them!

Tony Robbins used to hold a seminar. I'm not sure if he still does this, but one of the exercises the participants perform is his famous fire walk, where the participants control their thoughts to the point that they believe that they are walking on 'cool moss' versus 'hot coals.' It sounds challenging, especially when you know it's not true.

If you focus 100% on something, no other thought can get into your consciousness. Therefore, the seed that you planted in your subconscious mind, that the coals were cool moss, grows and expands sufficiently that you can walk over hot coals without burning your feet or feeling the heat of the coals.

You can apply this to any unproductive thought. Your new empowering thoughts can smother the disempowering thoughts and begin to grow. When you get a disempowering thought, take the opposite empowering thought and create a powerful vision statement. Memorize this powerful vision statement and repeat it as often as possible. Repeat it regularly over and over again. Concentrate the thought so intensely that the negative, disempowering thought gets smothered and dies, leaving fertile ground for your empowering thought to grow and eventually become a solid belief within your subconscious.

When you concentrate on thought this way, the effect is as apparent as a magnifying glass focusing on the sun's power.

You must eliminate or avoid the negativity of others as well. When others present negativity, focus on the bright side of the issuer situation, and when appropriate, change the subject to something pleasant. Don't be afraid to remove yourself from negative people or situations when your presence isn't necessary. Ensure that your thoughts get back on track with positivity.

Additionally, ensure that your predominant mental attitude is consistent with the perfect, powerful, loving, strong, harmonious Spirit within you. You can't think all day negatively and then believe that one concentrated positive thought will work.

Ultimately, your thoughts are the actions you take that create the result or conditions in your outer world. Thoughts are the cause, and your outer world reality is the effect. This is the *Law of Cause and Effect*, the *Law of Attraction*, and is believed by many to be the origin of good and evil.

The perfect Spirit within you must relate your outer world conditions to your thoughts. Therefore, if your thoughts are perfect, strong, powerful, loving, and harmonious, the conditions in your outer world will match those thoughts. If your thoughts are faulty, weak, violent, hateful, and hostile, the conditions in your outer world will also match those thoughts.

Good and evil... your positive, loving thoughts are in harmony with the Universe, and your negative thoughts are your devil.

"As thy faith is, so be it unto thee."

Either way you look at it, the *Law of Attraction* or the power of prayer works.

Meditation Exercise Nine

Visualize a 500-year-old oak tree. Remember when the earth's ground in which the tree now stands was bare. See the tiny plant burst through the soil. It is now a living thing, something alive and beginning to search for the meaning of sustaining life. Plant an acorn in a spot, water it, care for it, and ensure that it gets the direct rays of the morning sun.

Now see yourself at the location in which the tree now stands. See the roots penetrating the earth, watch them shoot out in all directions, and remember that they are living cells dividing and subdividing and will soon number millions. Remember that each cell is intelligent and knows what it wants and how to get it. See the stem shoot forward and upward. Watch it divide and form branches. See how perfect and symmetrical each branch is formed. See the leaves begin to develop, and as you watch, a giant beauty of nature unfolds perfectly. If you concentrate intently, you will become conscious of its smell. You can smell the leaves as the breeze gently sways the beautiful creation you have visualized.

Now see the branches divide and subdivide as the magnificent tree overwhelms the acorns beneath it. See the sunset and winter come. Watch the leaves turn colors and fall to the ground as this magnificent giant looks vulnerable to the world. See springtime buds begin to form as life begins to be evident and the breath of life consumes the tree, while you know that every intelligent cell knows how to attract what it needs to live in perfect harmony with the Universe.

When you can make your vision clear and complete, you will be able to enter into the spirit of a thing. It will become very real to you. You will be learning to concentrate. The process is the same whether you are focused on health, a grand oak tree, an ideal, a complicated business proposition, or any other life problem.

Nothing Happens by Accident

Chapter Ten

Nothing happens by accident. There is a cause for all things that occur. You co-create your future when you learn how to control any situation by bringing appropriate causes into action. You can continue to live your life, allowing unknown causes to create effects and be governed by your feelings and emotions as they happen without conscious interpretation, or you can decide to design your destiny.

You can no longer make excuses or blame anything or anyone else for your lack of results or the unfavorable circumstance that you find yourself in. You will know that the Universe has responded to your command.

The natural laws of the Universe govern cause and effect. Cause and effect occur in our inner and outer worlds, based on this natural law itself and the Spiritual Power, with unlimited resources, behind the law.

We live in an abundant Universe. All you must do is look around. Nature is bountiful and excessive in everything. Everything from plants to animals reproduces abundantly and continues to create and recreate in excess. No conservation efforts occur naturally in anything that is created.

Yet, the dirt and ground on our earth are lifeless and cannot create life. Never has the soil and land created life, and they never will. Not a single atom of our mineral world can ever create life. No evidence anywhere in the Universe proves that life has ever or ever will be created by anything other than life itself. At the point of life's first existence, science has no explanation.

When you plant an acorn, and the roots begin to grow, they reach into the mineral world, and there is life. The soil is useless without the acorn from a living tree. Once the acorn is seated in this lifeless soil, a suitable environment miraculously develops as the *Law of Growth* begins to take effect. The acorn sprouts the roots that create life into the otherwise dead soil. As the acorn's roots grow, we see the first sign of life being created as it breaks through the earth's crust, and an oak tree unfolds before us.

Similarly, the individual is lifeless. It is the Spirit that gives us life. Universal Energy reaches down into the human mind and gives it life; our thoughts link us to the Infinite. Think about it. It's not as if we can reach up and grab some spirit and put it into a stuffed animal to become alive. Without the Spirit, our bodies alone are lifeless.

When you plant a thought in the Universal Mind, the roots begin to grow. The thought is given life, and then amazingly results begin as the *Law of Growth* takes effect. As the thought continues to grow in the Universal Mind, we begin to see the first sign as the creation breaks through the barrier between the inner and outer worlds as the evidence of your thought begins to unfold in your outer world.

Thought is a powerful form of dynamic energy that aligns with its object and brings it from the inner world to the outer world. This is the law in which all things are created.

They are first created in thought and then realized in our physical world by the power of the Infinite.

Now make sure to distinguish creation from evolution. Creation is quite different. Creation is something new, bringing into the physical world something that currently does not exist. Evolution is a change involving things that already exist in the physical world.

You have the power within to co-create. You think it and then allow the Infinite to create it. 'Decree a thing, and it shall be established unto thee.' However, this power does not form the physical being that you are. It is the power of the Creator. As Jesus said, *"It is not I that doeth the works, but the Father that dwelleth within me, He doeth the work."*

You don't have the power to influence universal laws or to assist these laws in bringing about creation. You comply with the law, and the All-Powerful will bring about the result of your thoughts.

Your objective must be to imagine the perfect picture of the desired result. Don't worry whether you have the intelligence or a well-thought-out, detailed plan to bring about your desires. The Infinite with unlimited resources can be depended upon to find the best way to bring about the desired result, and you will be presented with what is needed when needed.

Electricity, cellular service, satellites, and radio waves are all energies, currents, or vibrations. They are invisible, yet they each have laws that apply to them that make them work. You may not understand how these laws work, but that's irrelevant to those who desire to benefit from them. Your objective is to learn how to operate within the laws that govern these objects.

How do you live in harmony with a law unless you know what the law is? Most of our fabulous inventions required observations and trial and error. Over and over again they test this and that, and eventually, the results showed clearly that the invention found a way to operate in harmony with the laws that govern these invisible powers.

Likewise, how do you know how to operate in harmony with natural, universal laws that bring about desired results and our outer world? Over and over again, test this and that, and eventually, the result clearly shows how to operate in harmony with the laws that govern the invisible spiritual power. Similarly, it is through observations and trial and error.

For more than 2000 years, great teachers have shared their observations. Nature has expressed itself constantly, and it is readily observable by all. Where there's growth, there must be life. This is indisputable. Where there is life, there must be harmony so that everything that has life constantly attains the conditions necessary for its complete expression.

Consider the waters of the ocean and the forest when left undisturbed. Life attracts the conditions and supply of whatever is needed to be abundant and fully expressed. Life seeks harmony to flourish.

When considering radio waves, harmony forms a circuit and allows the music being broadcasted to be heard miles away from the broadcast. You don't hear any music when the circuit is not formed; the result could be static or nothing.

Like the laws that allow radio waves to work, when your thoughts are in harmony with the principles of nature or the Infinite Mind, you operate in vibrational alignment, and the circuit is formed. You receive the benefits of what is being broadcast. When the circuit is not formed, or when you're not operating within these principles, you don't receive the benefit of what's being broadcast.

If your thoughts are not harmonious with the Infinite, you will not create the circuit, and your thoughts will remain with you. Thoughts that remain with you in this regard are not healthy and bring about worry, doubt, and fear.

As a result, the solar plexus contracts and cannot radiate the energy to your muscles and nerves, which ultimately is unhealthy.

Therefore, your creative thoughts must be harmonious to create abundance in the outer world. Thoughts that are not harmonious are destructive to you unless eliminated.

"Never talk defeat. Use words like hope, belief, faith, and victory."

~Norman Vincent Peale

Ultimately, all harmonious conditions result from the power that comes from within. You develop power by practice. The more you consciously control your thoughts to think only harmonious thoughts consistent with the natural principles of the Infinite, the more power you develop and the more you can co-create everything you desire. The objective, then, would be to develop power.

Meditation Exercise Ten

Abundance won't drop in your lap out of the clear blue sky. You must act. The conscious realization of the *Law of Action* and operating in harmony with the Infinite will materialize your desire.

> *"It's not enough to know what to do; you must do what you know."*
>
> ~Tammy Gallagher

Take your position and select a blank space on the wall, and mentally draw a black horizontal line about 6 inches long. See the line as plainly as though it were painted on the wall. Now mentally draw two vertical lines connecting with the horizontal line at both ends. Now draw another horizontal line connecting the ends of the two vertical lines. You now have a rectangle. Make all of the lines the same length. You now have a square.

See the square perfectly. Then draw a large circle within the square. Place a point in the center of the circle and draw the point toward you about 10 inches. You should be visualizing a cone on a square base.

Change the color of your lines from black to white, then red, then yellow. Now change the color of the entire drawing to orange. Make it three dimensional and rotate the cone so you can picture it standing on its base. If you can do this, you are making excellent progress and will soon be able to concentrate on any situation you desire.

Faith Will Deliver Miracles

Chapter 11

We all know people who have achieved amazing things. They have changed everything in their lives, and mainly they have changed themselves. We may call this a fantastic transformation or a miracle. However, all required to bring about this level of achievement, or transformation, is an understanding of the truth of the power of prayer or the *Law of Attraction*.

This powerful law eliminates the uncertainty in our lives and provides us with consistent predetermined results every time. You are fortunate to be here in this place and time in which this power within you has been recognized and realized throughout every civilized nation in the world. Many are attaining results through a process that they don't even understand.

If you were to eliminate free will or your ability to choose consciously, what results would you realize with the *Law of attraction*? And why do opposites attract? How does all this fit together?

Let's ponder the Universe itself. By what means is everything in the Universe kept together? When we consider magnetic forces, opposites attract, and like forces need their distance from each other. This distance among like forces seems to keep stars, and other planets at a sufficient distance from each other and, in turn, keeps the Universe in harmony.

On the other hand, we tend to see opposites in people attract. We see it regularly in business relationships or personal relationships. People with nothing in common seem to develop better relationships than those with much. Why is that so?

In a business partnership, if both partners bring precisely the same personal attributes and strengths, one of the partners would be unnecessary. We tend to have demands for what we do not possess. This is the *Law of Supply and Demand.*

A disturbance is observed in the motion of Uranus, and another star is needed to keep the solar system in place. Neptune arrives precisely on schedule. Where there is a demand, supply is created. This well-defined need or demand receives its solution by natural law. It attracts what it needs almost instantly.

In this example, no thought occurs. Its intelligence results in precisely the perfect outcome every time. With us, however, we can choose what we desire and therefore create different results. Our choices tend to focus on something that will complete us somehow. We have a demand, and the unlimited resources of the Infinite provides the supply.

The choice is a result of a thought that is active and creative. Through our thoughts, things can be created, and this creation in our mind ultimately creates here on earth. Once your thoughts break through you, becoming a part of your subconscious and therefore united with the Infinite, they pass from truth to truth in the eternal light, where all of this is, was, or ever shall be, is harmonized.

From your silent reflection and contemplation, you become inspired. This inspiration comes from the Divine source and the inception of a new creation, or demand, in your mind. The Divine is creative and intelligent, superior to all other external forces, and therefore can understand and possess every element of your outer world.

Thought is the most remarkable, most powerful finding of all time. This intelligent, creative power takes your ideas and makes them live in the outer world. Jesus said, *"What things soever you desire, when ye pray, believe that ye receive them, and ye shall have them."*

Those who have mastered this understanding seem to have everything come to them so easily. They never appear to have difficulty, and it's as if everything goes right for them all the time. They always seem happy and live perfectly with themselves and the Universe.

At the moment you believe that your desire has already been fulfilled, you are planting the seed of thought of absolute perfection, eliminating any limitations. The seed, if left undisturbed, will germinate in your outer world reality as the forces are set in motion to bring it about in your outer world.

Technology has given us the ability to connect with millions today. To be able to pass on this simple but powerful truth to so many more than ever before, placing us in a unique point in time that is more wonderful than ever dreamed of by most. Regardless of your perspective, there is the same underlying truth.

- Jesus said, *"Believe that ye receive, and ye shall receive."*
- Paul said, *"Faith is the substance of things hoped for, the evidence of things not seen."*
- The *Law of Attraction* is the law by which thought correlates with its object.

All three statements result in the same outcome or the exact cause and effect. They are just different perspectives of the same truth. This does not mean there is no truth to any of these statements. It simply better defines it and shows how it is being held concerning our needs and becoming more understood. Truth's completeness requires a variety of perspectives and is not limited to only one perspective.

Which perspective resonates with you is irrelevant. They all mean that when you learn to impress upon the Universal Mind the image showing that your desire is already an existing fact, and you do so without doubt or reservation, you have mastered the power of your creative thought. You will know how to use the power to solve every problem you ever have, and the Universe will apply this to your demand. You will have realized the marvelous gift given to all by God.

Meditation Exercise Eleven

In this exercise, you are going to do something a little different. Take your meditation position, and still your body and mind, then relax your body and mind. Inhibit thought.

Now concentrate on the following quote from the Bible: "Whatsoever things ye desire, when ye pray, believe that you receive them and ye shall have them."

Make sure that there are no limitations when you focus on this statement. 'Whatsoever things' is obvious and implies that the only limitation is those we place upon ourselves through our thoughts. Remember that faith is the essence of things hoped for, the evidence of things not seen.

God's Gift of

Thought

Chapter Twelve

God's gift of thought, and therefore, the power to create, has been given to everyone and is unlimited. Creation is our Divine purpose. The creative power we all have within us due to our unity with the Infinite gives us independence and freedom.

You can co-create an ideal situation in your business life, at home, and with your friends and acquaintances without regard to resources or costs. The omnipotence of your thought will draw upon the unlimited resources of the Infinite, and all that you need will be at your command.

There are three steps to ensure that you attract what you desire.

- It is essential first to understand the power of the Spirit within.
- You must then have the courage to act.
- Finally, you must have faith to allow it to happen.

"To one who has faith, no explanation is necessary. To one without faith, no explanation is possible."

~Saint Thomas Aquinas

All power comes from the Spirit within, and through tranquility and the stillness of the mind, you unite with the omnipotent power of the Infinite through your subconscious mind.

If you desire power, wisdom, or permanent success in any regard, you will find it only within. Understand that only in absolute silence may you come in contact with Divinity. A silent, still mind is not an easy feat, so persistent practice is necessary, and your reward will lead to power. This power will increase as you become more proficient in using it. More importantly, the power is permanent and carries no adverse conditions, providing long-term results when used.

Everything that is created is created in consciousness first. By governing your thoughts today, you shape your future events and environment. Feelings of love united with your desires, and the proper education, is the most potent combination with the *Law of Attraction.*

To some, this concept is entirely different from what they've been taught, and it isn't easy to comprehend. Why is it so difficult to accept a new idea? Change seems painful as we venture into something we've never experienced before. In most cases, we are conditioned, and our minds cannot comprehend something entirely new until we are prepared to receive it.

You must create the necessary brain cells through a concentrated focus, which will be ready to receive the omnipotence of the *Law of Attraction,* enabling you to comprehend the unlimited power that's within you. You must become a vibrational match.

Once you have come to a proper understanding of the power within you, then you must act upon it. It is evident that we attract what we focus on, yet somehow, we still have doubts, fears, anxiety, or worry. Like all negative thoughts, these disempowering thoughts stay with us and keep our desires further away from us. All disempowering thoughts are not in harmony with the Universe and remain with you. They cannot be united with the Universal Mind. These disempowering thoughts linger with you, and ultimately, you reap what you sow.

Therefore, if you think disempowering thoughts more often than empowering, you keep pushing away those things you desire.

A thought will correlate with its object and will be delivered to you in the physical world as long as your thoughts are in harmony with the Universe. Being in harmony with the Universe requires that your thoughts carry truth. This harmony is what allows the *Law of Growth* to manifest your thoughts.

The *Law of Attraction*, or the power of prayer, gives thought the power to correlate with its object and, ultimately, to master every adverse condition you face. Love conveys life into thought. Any thought that is permeated with love is unconquerable. The Infinite is intelligent. But it is also energy. This energy gets its vitality from the feelings generated by love and is the force that brings electrons together by the *Law of Attraction* so that they can form atoms. The atoms are energized together and form molecules, which take the form of the material objects of our desire.

The feelings generated by love are the creative force that sparks the chain of events that ultimately results in your desires being manifested. The combination of thought brought alive with love creates the unconquerable cause that the *Law of Attraction* has a constructive effect.

All universal laws are unconquerable: electricity, radio waves, cellular signals, and gravitation. Cellular phones are common today. However, when you're talking on a cellular phone and your phone call is dropped, you don't blame the natural law that allows cellular signals to operate cell phones. You know that something is blocking the signal. Similarly, you cannot blame the *Law of Attraction* for not delivering your desired result. You cannot blame God for not answering your prayers. Instead, we must look at the aspects within our control. It will likely be something as simple as needing to understand the application that caused the lack of our desires to manifest.

Define your ideal picture or vision clearly. The end picture must be precisely concluded. You don't have to worry about the details associated with how you get to the result or perfect picture. The Universe has the resources to fill in the gaps more adequately than you do, so focus on the detailed result. Not only must it be defined, but it must be consistent. Changing your perfect picture weekly will not create the subconscious realization of your desire.

An architect started working on plans, and the picture in his mind's eye was of a two-story contemporary home but the next week he decided to change it to a traditional ranch. The following week, he thought he might be better with a Tudor-style home. When do you think he'll finish the plans, and what would the end plan look like? Would you have a clear set of plans by the end of the third week? It's not likely. Therefore, plans can only begin to be finalized with a clear result, or the things you desire will be continually delayed and fragmented.

You do this consistently if you direct concentrated thought without other thoughts interrupting you. In that case, you will be delivered powerful results, and your desires will be created in your reality.

Meditation Exercise Twelve

In your usual meditation place, relax and let go, mentally and physically. Always do this and never try to do any mental work under pressure. Ensure that there are no tense muscles or nerves and that you are entirely comfortable. Now realize your unity with the Infinite. Get in touch with this power. Come into deep and vital understanding, appreciation, and realization that your ability to think is your ability to act upon the Universal Mind and bring it into manifestation.

Realize that the power of the Divine will meet every requirement and that you already have the same potential ability that any individual has ever had or ever will have because each of us is an expression or manifestation of the Infinite. All of us are parts of the whole. There is no difference in kind or quality. The only difference is of degree.

The Father and I Are One

Chapter Thirteen

Some people hold extraordinary spiritual capabilities yet are often brushed off and not accepted as people with true spiritual power. Without scientific proof, many in our society find it difficult to believe anything. However, inductive reasoning has been used repeatedly to prove the truth. Yet, resistance is still related to the spiritual power of thought.

Some conclude that there are people who hold supernatural powers for which there is no explanation. However, just because there's no explanation doesn't mean there's no truth to these powers. Inductive reasoning is convincing that every phenomenon results from a definite cause and natural law or principle that operates with precision every time.

The inductive science of careful repeated observations in many circumstances concludes that there are many occurrences whose internal operations we don't understand. Yet, the principle by which the occurrence operates is consistent and reliable.

Some believe that these unexplained occurrences are things we should leave alone. But if you look throughout time, many of our advances and knowledge have been a direct result of someone boldly questioning what was perceived by some as 'forbidden ground.'

Inductive science confirms that thought is spiritual, creative, and powerful. Thought, when consciously directed toward empowering beliefs of faith, courage, and enthusiasm, is the spiritual power tool we all have been given to achieve our desires.

Our predominant mental attitude sets the stage for every condition we experience. Empowering thoughts will result in pleasant circumstances, just as disempowering thoughts will result in unpleasant circumstances. If you fear tragedy and therefore focus on it, tragedy will result. If your predominant thoughts are upon joy, joy will be delivered.

One challenge is that many things we focus on don't give us the satisfaction we thought they would once we get them, or they provide only temporary satisfaction. The Universal Mind does not decide whether what we focus on is going to satisfy us or not; it simply delivers to us that in which we believe.

Ask yourself, what do you want in life? What do you want? Don't answer this from a micro perspective. Answer it from a macro perspective.

It is likely that everyone, yes, everyone, wants the same thing, and that's happiness and harmony. If we're happy, we have everything we want or need, and if we're happy, we have more of ourselves to give.

"Remember, happiness doesn't depend upon who you are or what you have; it depends solely upon what you think."

~Dale Carnegie

To be happy, most of us would agree that we would want to be in excellent health, have harmonious, exciting, loving relationships, and have an abundant supply of all the material items we desire. If you throw away all limitations, you want the best of everything.

Would you be happy if you were healthy, had great, harmonious, exciting, loving relationships, and had an abundant supply of all the material items you desire?

Jesus said, *"Father and I are one."* The Father is our creator and the original substance from which all things are made. The concept of the Father within you has been taught for over 2000 years. It is the core belief of almost every system of philosophy or religion and can pretty much be considered truth among the majority.

So how is it that we get the tangible results of health, love, and wealth that the Father, our Creator within us, is capable of delivering to anyone and everyone? Through our creative power of thought. Thought is our spiritual power. It is the explanation for every condition or circumstance. The day of the dreamer has come.

Recognize that it's not enough to know what to do. You must do what you know. Nothing is ever accomplished by knowledge alone. The phrase 'knowledge is power' is not entirely accurate. The improved statement is that 'knowledge and thought put into action is power.' Thoughts are the cause, and your circumstance is the effect. Empowering thoughts of courage, love, health, or caring for others set causes in motion to deliver the desired effects. It's as simple as giving mentally.

An unhappy thought cannot exist in a happy state of mind. Staying focused on the thoughts that make you feel happy and good is necessary to place the *Law of Attraction* into action in your life. Remember also that you are a finite being with limited resources. Yet the Infinite is limitless with infinite resources. You are to therefore create a mental image of your perfect outcome without predetermining the path on which you will get there. Allow the Infinite's unlimited resources to present the proper path.

"When one has made one's demands upon the universal, one must be ready for surprises.

Everything may seem to be going wrong when in reality, it is going right."

~Florence Scovel Shin

By detaching yourself from the path to your perfect outcome, you allow the Infinite resources to find the most efficient path. This may, at times, present you with what appears to be chaos or unexpected circumstances. However, have faith that the path will deliver your desired outcome. Listen to your inner voice and focus on your desired outcome; your feelings will guide you appropriately.

When creating your perfect picture in your mind's eye, also remember that you must focus on how you want to feel in the perfect situation. Remaining focused on how you feel always allows the Infinite to fill in the gaps with the most efficient and effective means, to deliver the conditions and feelings you created in your mind.

Through the *Law of Causation*, dreamers bring their desires into their reality. When you begin to unconsciously come into the understanding of this tremendous realization that you are part of the whole, and the spirit within you is truly united with the Divine, that you are one with the creator and the same in quality and kind, that 'The Father and I are one,' then you will understand the transcendental possibilities that are at your command.

Meditation Exercise Thirteen

This lesson is simple but powerful. Take your position and still your body and mind, then relax your body and mind, and inhibit thought. Now, recognize that you are a part of the whole and that 'The Father and I are one,' is a true statement for you. A part must be the same in kind and quality as the whole, with the only difference being degree. You can become a vessel by which the Infinite can answer your prayers and bring about the realization of your desire.

The Uncertainty Principle

Chapter Fourteen

You have learned that your outer world is controlled by an unexplainable power universally accepted as God and that we are all united with this All-Powerful source. You'll also learn that thought is a creative spiritual process, and it is powerful. This power, however, doesn't originate within you but from the Infinite channeled through you.

You understand that the conscious and subconscious minds work together as one mind. The conscious mind directs the subconscious by creating beliefs for the subconscious to act upon. The subconscious mind is united with the Universal Mind, and this unity allows us access to all power and the unlimited resources of the Infinite.

How does all of this relate to science or, better yet, to physics? The answer will amaze you. When I first learned of the uncertainty principle in 2007, it seemed outrageous to comprehend.

Let's first review the makeup of all matter. Matter comprises molecules, which are made of atoms and electrons. In physics, an uncertainty principle concludes that there is no guarantee about the pattern of electrons. When looking at the probability that an electron will arrive in a given circumstance, the conclusion is that it is impossible to predict precisely what will happen.[12] Only the odds can be predicted. Physics has given up on finding a solution to this unpredictability. Yes! Physics has given up. Science has given up.

Even more mind boggling is that the predictability of electrons changes when electrons are observed.[12] It is suspected that it will be impossible ever to find the answer to this mystery and accept it as nature really is. Some physicists believe that electrons have and internal variable that science isn't aware of, possibly that is why it cannot be predicted. They believe that this internal variable is thought—human thought.

Yes, thought could be the variable that will change the outcome of how electrons respond. Electrons don't form atoms, which won't form molecules and will not unite with other molecules to form matter if it weren't for thought. Without thought intervention, electrons would remain without assembling into atoms and molecules. How can this be? What happens to the electrons when we're not observing them if they don't assemble into atoms, which ultimately make up matter?

The Infinite Energy, in which we are all united, is also united with electrons, and this may very well be the cause behind electrons assembling when thought is present versus when it is not. This is mind-boggling to me. For example, the electrons of a ball are not in the shape of a ball unless there is an observer who knows it's a ball. Knowing it's a ball is gained through the individual's unity with the Universal Mind. This explains how we manifest our thoughts and beliefs into reality. Electrons have the same potential speed as all other cosmic energy, such as light, electricity, and thought. Light travels about 186,000 miles a second. In essence, electrons travel similarly to the speed of light and likely faster. They can assemble almost instantaneously when they are within our site. And, due to our limited capabilities, and the speed in which electrons travel, this assemblage happens without us being able to see it happening.

Electrons fill all space and are ultimately everywhere, even what appears to be empty. So, in essence, electrons make up everything in our physical world and could be considered the Universal Substance from which all material things are made. If electrons are the Universal Substance, then the Infinite permeates electrons.

All things originate in thought and appear physically due to thought-directing electrons. That same power can also eliminate things. It is thought that gives all matter forms in our physical world.

For every effect, there is a cause. If we follow the trail of every effect backward in time, we will find the creative thought from which the effect grew.

Let's look at how all of this relates to our bodies. Every part of our body is made up of cells. Some of these cells rely upon each other, and some are independent. All cells have enough intelligence to perform all functions they are required to perform. All cells are intelligent enough to ensure their future existence. These cells choose what they need and what they don't need. Each cell is born, reproduces itself, dies, and is absorbed. Life itself requires the continuous renewal of these cells.

The mind of our cells is that of our subconscious mind. Cells act without thought or conscious knowledge and are responsive to the will of our conscious mind. This is the explanation for metaphysical healing. The power of a belief in the subconscious mind also provides the manifestations as it relates to our bodies.

God is Infinite, has unlimited resources, and is omnipresent. Therefore, we must be an expression or manifestation of this All-Powerful Mind. Our subconscious, which gives intelligence to our cells, is united with God's mind, the Universal Mind, which is united with intelligence and electrons, and so on. The All-Powerful Universal Mind is in everything and everyone; the resources available to us through this unity are limitless, and what gives creative thought so much power.

Your subconscious mind is the link between your conscious mind, your mental world, and the Universal Mind of the spiritual world. You have direct access to God or the Infinite. It is, therefore, evident that no limits can be placed upon the power of thought when in alignment with all that is good. Do you realize that recognizing this fact places you in touch with Omnipotence?

Thoughts, faith, alignment with the Universe, and all that is good will manifest every time. Thoughts that are disempowering and not aligned with the Universe will stay with you and can never enter the vibrational force of Eternal Energy. They will deliver negative results. Understanding this principle explains the power of prayer.

We need to think and pray correctly. Thought creates our beliefs, and this is the only reality that will ever manifest. Thoughts with faith, are like prayers with faith. Thoughts will only materialize with faith. Conditions and circumstances in our physical world are outward manifestations of thought. If we change our thoughts and beliefs, we change our material conditions, as conditions must be in harmony with their creator. And our thoughts unite with the Universal Mind through our subconscious mind.

When our thoughts have faith and conviction and are in harmony with the Infinite, we will achieve what we believe and can conceive every time.

So here is the secret: thought must be empowering, focused, defined, consistent, and aligned with the universal good. You can't spend a lifetime thinking negatively and expect 20 to 30 minutes a day of positive thinking to work overnight.

If you decide today to be disciplined, you must ensure that nothing interferes with your decision. This decision to change the way you think is the decision to change your life. Not only will you bring about benefits and material things, but you will also experience more love and physical health.

Who you are is a reflection of your thoughts and beliefs. It's your character, your environment, and even your appearance. To change who you are, you must change how you think.

Meditation Exercise Fourteen

In your position, as usual, completely relax. Concentrate on harmony, which means with all that the word implies. Concentrate so profoundly and intently that you will be conscious of nothing but harmony. Remember, we learn by doing. Reading these lessons is only the start. Action and practical application are what will create results.

The Importance of Words

Chapter Fifteen

Universal laws, when understood and applied properly, consistently work to your advantage and are always in process.

The Eternal Energy that sets the forces in motion to deliver what you desire and picture perfectly in your mind's eye needs your imagination and for you to operate in harmony with all that is good. Anytime you're not in harmony with the Infinite, you are either refusing to release something you no longer need or refusing to accept something you require.

We grow by exchanging the old for the new, the good for the improved. You can't get what you lack if you keep holding on to what you have.

Your ability to take from each experience only what you need while releasing what you don't need will determine the degree of harmony and happiness you'll attain.

As you expand your visions and ascend to greater levels of awareness, you improve your ability to understand your true desires and what you are to focus on to attract what you need to attain them.

Everything that happens to you occurs for your benefit. When the things that come to you are not the things that you want, then it's because you somehow haven't learned what you are supposed to do, and until you do, you will continue to have circumstances that you don't want.

To grow, you must become in consciousness what you want to attract. You must behave the way you want to be treated. You know the golden rule. 'Do unto others as you would have them do unto you.'

Ultimately, understanding the universal laws and applying them will ensure your desired outcome and happiness. The universal *Law of Reciprocity* states that you benefit in an expanded proportion to your effort. The effort you put forth now to understand universal laws will reward you with happiness in the future.

For your thoughts to have vitality or life, they must be drenched with love. Since love is a strong emotion, your thoughts must be guided by reason but filled with love. Love gives thoughts life and allows it to grow. The *Law of Attraction* doesn't work for thoughts that aren't filled with love.

Thought expresses itself in physical form, and all your thoughts lead to some effect. This makes it evident that you can think only positive thoughts and thoughts consistent with your true desires.

Thoughts are often expressed through the words we use, even when the words are in our heads. It is essential that you use only empowering words that align with the abundance you desire in your life, as your mind's eye visualizes by mirroring the words you use.

The correct choice of words will lead to improved pictures in your mind. The more you clearly define these things through proper words, the more clearly defined your pictures become.

Our ability to formulate thought through words makes us different from any other animal that walks the earth. Words create mental pictures that are eternal and allow us to pass on eternal knowledge and document history. They allow us to visualize our future to influence its outcome. Words allow us to create visions and dreams of the future.

We have been able to record the greatest thinkers and writers of all time, and this record is that of Universal Thought taking form in the minds of individuals. These individuals act as messengers.

Words are a form of thought that express themselves in form. The unity of all harmonious thought or Universal Thought is the Creator, and this thought manifests through individual thought. Therefore, we must choose our words carefully.

Words are a means by which the Universe gives us access to unlimited resources. When in alignment with all that is good, our word expressions enter the well-being stream and materialize.

Principles are the backbone of mathematics, health, light, truth, and abundance. It is no surprise that principle exists in thought. A thought with vitality has principle, and vitality gives thought power.

We know this is true because we are sure of the result when we apply the principle correctly. For example, the darkness is no longer there when we shine light in a room. When we tell the truth, we can't be dishonest.

These are indisputable facts. Just like vital thoughts contain principle, life, and lives by the *Law of Growth*. Vital thoughts take root and smother negative thoughts. Negative thoughts, by their nature, contain no vitality.

This fact, which continues to show true every time, enables you to destroy all negativism, lack, and limitation. If you understand the creative power of thought, you master your destiny.

The appearance of a given amount of energy anywhere means the disappearance of the same amount somewhere else. We can receive only what we give away. Therefore, we don't want to give others what we don't wish upon ourselves.

Meditation Exercise Fifteen

Insight is something that we attain and develop. It is essential to any outstanding achievement and is obtained through silent reflection and concentration. It allows us to be prepared for obstacles before we ever experience them. Insight paves the road in front of us that permits us to develop plans in the right direction.

This exercise has you concentrating on insight. In meditation, focus the thought on the fact that knowing the creative power of thought is significantly more potent than possessing the ability to think. Let the thought dwell on the fact that knowledge does not apply itself. Your actions are not governed by knowledge but by custom, precedent, and habit. The only way you can get yourself to apply knowledge is by a determined conscious effort.

Call to mind the fact that unused knowledge is forgotten and that the value of the information is in applying the principle. Continue this line of thought until you gain sufficient insight to formulate a definite program for applying this principle to a particular circumstance, challenge, or opportunity.

Specifically, concentrate on a goal that you already have the knowledge needed. You've had this knowledge, but have you applied it? Get creative and concentrate on using this knowledge and putting it into action through the conscious creative effort of thought. It is not enough to know what to do; you must do what you know.

What is Your Purpose?

Chapter Sixteen

Most agree that wealth, health, and love are the three predominant characteristics that, when acquired, can add to your happiness and success in your outer world.

Financial wealth can be described as the possession of things that provide exchange value. It is an effect, however, not a cause. It is the result of your actions and provides a means for you to continue to create. It should never be desired as an end but as a means of accomplishing your desires.

Success is not financial wealth but a higher ideal with a definite purpose. To truly attain financial wealth, you must have a definite purpose or ideal that benefits more than just you. With a definite purpose, the means and abundance will be provided.

Spend some time right now and ask this question of yourself. What is your definite purpose or ideal? Consider what you do every day that benefits others. If you are unsatisfied with your answer, concentrate on what you want to bring to others. How can you maximize benefits to all in what you enjoy doing every day?

Great fortune comes from spiritual power. There are many clear examples. Think of those whom you consider your heroes in life. Were they given everything? Were they given anything of significance? Did they attract their wealth because of their purpose in life?

> *"Nothing splendid has ever been achieved except by those who dared to believe that something inside of them was superior to circumstance."*
>
> ~ Bruce Barton

Your higher purpose will bring about true lasting wealth. Universal laws work perfectly and harmoniously when an ideal with a higher purpose is your focus. It's as if everything seems to fall into place.

You can use your own experiences as evidence of this fact. Just compare your results in life when your desires and actions were focused on high ideals to the benefit of all versus the times when you had selfish desires or ulterior motives.

We all know people who have fortunes but didn't have to do a thing for them, and we ask, how did this happen? What's their higher purpose? They didn't 'earn' their fortune, and they certainly don't use it for the benefit of a higher ideal.

Keep in mind that this artificial wealth is likely limited or will be lost. You can't have true wealth that is long-lasting if you don't earn it based on an ideal that benefits more than just yourself.

You can see this play out often in business. Most truly successful business people are idealists who continue to strive to be better or for better ways of accomplishing things. They don't allow the current standards to run their businesses, and they run their businesses with high moral and ethical standards to sustain their success.

It's also wise to understand that financial wealth's real value is not in the things you have or the amount of money in your bank account but in spending or exchanging what you have for something different and new, for something that allows your creative spiritual power to take root.

All creation is a result of spiritual power, nothing else, and there are three simple yet complex steps to apply this power: idealization, visualization, and materialization.

Hold the perfect picture in your mind to bring about a different result in your life until your vision has been manifested. Don't worry or give thought to any outer world situations, as they are irrelevant in the perfect idealism within your mind. Just picture the result as you desire it to be without limitations.

It may not be easy to understand how thinking a thing will bring it to occur, but it is a scientific fact that it will manifest. Feel free to bring the 'how' it works into your current belief system any way you desire. The 'how' can be believed that God or Jesus delivers to you what you are worthy of, what you have risen in consciousness to know He will deliver.

Don't be overly concerned about how this works. Be reassured it works. We may never prove in this lifetime how it works. Just have faith, know that it works every time, and allow it to work for you.

Understand that you cannot experience something in your outer world if it isn't a condition you have in your inner world. Therefore, your success depends upon what you can vividly imagine in your mind's eye as an end desired result.

Every experience you have is a result of preceding thought. There are no coincidences in life, just as there's no such thing as being lucky or unlucky. All your circumstances are a result of clearly defined thought.

Thought is what changes your life's perceptions. And perception is your reality. Whatever you experience, everything you say, think, see, and feel becomes an impression and mental image influencing your beliefs. Yet you can also create your mental images without having to have experienced them. Regardless of circumstance, environment, or external sources, your thoughts can be the source of your mental pictures. This ability gives you the power to control your destiny.

It is the application of this power that allows you to determine your fate. When you consciously realize a condition in your mind's eye, that condition will manifest in your life. 'Thinking is the one great cause in life.' Therefore, controlling your thoughts allows you to control your destiny.

Thoughts must be formed precisely as you desire the result. The greater the feeling and love for others within your thoughts, the more vitality they are given. The vitality given by love will affect the speed at which your seed of thought will grow and manifest.

Consider three characteristics of thought: form, quality, and vitality. The form of your thought is one of clarity and boldness of the images you create in your mind's eye. The quality of your thought depends upon the substance. Meaning it depends upon the purpose and how much courage, determination, and vigor your thoughts hold. The amount of feeling within them determines the vitality of your thoughts. The more feeling of love for others in your thoughts, the greater the vitality. This gives thought life and allows it to grow and expand.

Constructive, harmonious thoughts always manifest positive results through the *Laws of Love, Attraction, and Growth*. Destructive thoughts that are not harmonious stick with you, and results follow these destructive thoughts, bringing evil and disease into your life.

Destructive thoughts won't grow outside you. They eventually will die within you and often kill a part of you in the process. Destructive thoughts are often referred to as evil. When we bring evil upon ourselves, it is simply our environment and body acting in equilibrium with our minds. It is neither good nor bad; it simply is. The body follows the mind, and our outer world can only mirror our inner world.

Your devil is your destructive thoughts, and evil is simply a word that describes your actions and outcomes resulting from your disempowering thoughts. Among all things, destructive thought must be eliminated.

The way you are guaranteed success is to focus on constructive thoughts. By visualizing your desire, form a mental picture in your mind's eye. By doing so, you will bring it about.

When you visualize, you are experiencing what already exists in the spiritual world. If you are faithful to your ideal, the visualization will one day appear in your outer world. Visualization is a result of your imagination. By imagining things, you impress upon the mind thoughts that form concepts and ideals, which are the plans from which the Master Architect designs your future.

"Your imagination is your preview of life's coming attractions."

~Albert Einstein

Feeling and thought in combination are irresistible. Some psychologists believe there is only one sense versus five or six. They believe that all senses are just modifications of the one sense of feeling. This supports why loving feelings gives life to thought. It is what gives thought power.

Visualization must be a conscious effort and represent exactly what you desire, versus a subconscious activity in which you realize whatever comes your way or images that represent your current belief system. Actual change in your life will only occur when you consciously direct your thoughts and mental images to the desired picture result.

Don't allow mental images that are not consciously directed and keep focused on your desires. Stay focused on the result – a farsighted vision of perfect resolution.

Meditation Exercise Sixteen

As always, take your position and relax your body and every muscle and nerve. Relax your mind and inhibit thought. Now bring yourself to a realization of the critical fact that harmony and happiness are states of consciousness and do not depend upon physical things.

Things are effects and come because of correct mental states. Therefore, if you desire material possessions of any kind, your chief concern should be to acquire the mental attitude that will bring about the desired result. This mental attitude is brought about by realizing your spiritual nature and your unity with the Infinite, which is the substance of all things. This realization will bring about everything necessary for your complete enjoyment. This is scientific and correct thinking.

When you succeed in bringing about this mental attitude, it is comparatively easy to realize your desire as an already accomplished fact. When you can do this, you will have found the 'truth' that makes you and everyone 'free' from every lack or limitation.

Concentrated Thought

Chapter Seventeen

You've heard the phrase 'man has dominion over all things,' haven't you? As you have learned, you do this through your thoughts. Thought is spiritual and united with the Infinite. Thought is the process that determines your circumstance every time.

You may be used to relying upon your five senses, but it is your 6th sense, your spiritual connection, in which all ideals are conceived. You can quickly obtain intuitive knowledge through a concentrated focus. The vibrations generated by your thought are what assemble the forces that provide the answers to all your questions.

Become conscious that your inner thoughts take hold of your Spirit. The Spirit of a thing is the thing itself. Without the Spirit or soul, the body is dead. The Spirit is a vital part of anything and is the aspect in which we are all connected. Your body is the outward vision of your Spirit, which is the case with all things. Therefore, thoughts focused inwardly speak to the Spirit, the soul of all things, united with everyone and everything. No wonder thoughts are so powerful.

When you consider all power within your control, mental power is superior to all other sources of power.

Most people spend years studying and working with numbers to ensure that they understand mathematics. Similarly, to understand the power of the mind, you will need to study and work with your mind and come to a conscious understanding of the omnipotence of your thoughts.

Your concentrated focus, as with anything, gets stronger with practice over time. Your continuous flow of thought, delivered persistently yet patiently, will provide the strength to plant the seeds that grow.

Think about an actor playing a role in a movie. You begin to understand the true talent of the best actors. They get so engrossed in their roles. They instinctively react and act as if they became the characters versus acting the parts. This is an excellent analogy for the definition of concentration. It is essential for you to become so interested in your thought, so immersed in your subject, that you can't be conscious of being anything else. It's as if you're already living the part.

Decide whom you want to be. Determine the role of the actor. Then play the part with everything you have. Become so immersed in your role that you leave the old you behind.

This level of concentration sets the forces of the Universal Mind in motion to deliver to you what you desire. You become a magnet.

"Whatever it is you envision for yourself, no matter how lofty or impossible it may seem to you right now, I encourage you to begin acting as if what you would like to become is already your reality. This is a wonderful way to set into motion the forces that will collaborate with you to make your dreams come true."

~ Doctor Wayne Dyer

When you instinctively begin to act the part, your subconscious mind already believes it to be true. When your subconscious has risen to what you desire, the evidence of your accomplishment will appear.

Concentration requires practice and, most importantly, an ability to control your mental and physical being. One of the keys is to stop focusing on what you want to have and focus on becoming whom you want to be. You cannot get the things you want until you become that person in consciousness.

An exceptional golfer focuses on the ball falling into the cup. Tiger Woods says, *"be the ball."* The result of this type of thinking is that there is a skill developed in getting the ball in the cup. A CEO of a successful company studies the area of their business and other businesses to envision and deliver a more successful company. Again, thinking in this regard will result in an improvement in the skills required to fulfill the needs of the company.

When we focus on anything other than being who we desire to be, the result is the opposite, and we become the person in the outer world that we are in our inner world.

You may have learned unintentionally to create what you do not want or to be something other than what you desire by thinking disempowering thoughts. Negative thoughts don't work toward achieving what you desire. They work against you.

Focusing on anything other than being the person you want to become will not deliver the desired result. This weakness impedes attaining the desired state of consciousness, and therefore, an impediment to accomplishing what you desire.

It is essential to become in consciousness the person you desire to be. This is accomplished much more quickly when the concentrated focus is mixed with a burning desire. The greater and more constant the desire, the more powerful the result.

When we look at many successful businesses and transactions with them, we find that the mental aspect of the business is the primary controlling factor. In other words, desire is the primary force. Your thoughts are to stay the course and be highly directed. Even in business, we can easily see that relationships and results are simply the externalizations of desire.

All of us are meant for greatness. It's within every one of us. However, the mind must develop the greatness that only can come from within. Your thoughts are what give you omnipotence. Physical effort doesn't come close to delivering the powerful results that your thoughts can deliver, as our thoughts channel all-natural power through our spiritual connection with the Divine.

The vibration created by a concentrated focus of thought connects with and attracts what's necessary to deliver your desires. Refrain from allowing the petty nonessential stuff to bog down your thoughts and impede your desired result.

Your mind must be strengthened to rise above the distractions of the day-to-day business and everyday happenings within your outer world.

There is nothing mysterious about it. When your thoughts are focused and persistent, they become identified with your vision. When you concentrate on a definite purpose, your subconscious will set forces in motion vibrationally to deliver to you the resources needed that will lead to success.

Once you plant the seed of thought, you must be ready for what presents itself to you. The Divine speaks to you intuitively. He reveals the truth you need precisely. It doesn't matter if you have the knowledge or experience that would typically be necessary. Your intuition will lead you to what you need.

Trust your intuition and work with it. Develop and nurture this power within you. Recognize and appreciate your intuition.

If you welcome, appreciate, and are thankful for what your intuition has given you, you will welcome His voice in the future. The more you welcome the insight delivered through your intuition, the more you recognize the gift of what is being presented, the more frequent His calls will become, and the more intuitive gifts you will receive.

Seek solitude frequently, as Divine inspiration usually appears in the silence. You don't need hours, just minutes daily. Step back, take a deep breath, and clear your mind.

Your intuition is a subconscious function, and the subconscious is omnipotent. Through your connection with the Infinite, your subconscious has unlimited resources and unlimited potential and power. However, a lack of desire can restrict and limit your access to these resources. You and your burning desire opens the door to Infinite resources. It is your lack of desire that limits access as well.

Your desire and predominant mental attitude are in direct proportion to the level of success you'll achieve. If you focus on a definite purpose, your subconscious will activate the Eternal Energy to deliver to you the resources needed to attract those things you demand.

The *Law of Love*, expressed through a definite purpose, positively serves others, and we earn happiness by serving others. Obtaining symbols of happiness, wealth, and power will ultimately be lost if they aren't earned by serving others.

You can only receive if you give—those who try to get without giving lose regardless.

Money has always been seen as a symbol of power. However, it should be seen only as the medium to accomplish your goals; it's a resource only. Those who are wealthy don't concern themselves with money. They have learned that money itself is not of importance. The actual importance is your purpose. With a definite purpose that serves others, all resources present themselves.

When your desire is in harmony with natural law, and you become so identified with the object of your thought that you are conscious of nothing else, then the invisible energy begins to be molded, which irresistibly brings you surroundings in correlation with your thought.

Meditation Exercise Seventeen

Relax the mind and body completely. Take the time you need to relax. Now concentrate on becoming in consciousness what you desire. Avoid any thoughts regarding your perception of outer world limitations. Remember that power comes through repose. Let the thought dwell upon your desire. Picture yourself being the person you desire until you completely identify with it and are conscious of nothing else.

If you wish to eliminate fear, concentrate on courage. If you wish to eliminate lack, concentrate on abundance. If you wish to eliminate disease, concentrate on health.

Visualize a situation where you will experience the opposite condition of what you want to be eliminated. See what you're wearing, the venue, the people around you, and your perfect performance. Create a faultless vision. Feel the way it would feel to be this person.

Always concentrate on the ideal as an already existing fact. This is the seed, the life principle that goes forth and creates those causes that guide, direct, and bring about the necessary relations, which eventually manifests in form.

You Are a Vessel for Divine Thought

Chapter Eighteen

Have you noticed the change? You know, the change that's occurring in the world today? Things are changing at the speed of light, or rather, the speed of thought. These changes affect everyone and everything and are beyond compare. As quickly as they are changing now, they will change in the future.

Sometimes we see thought and truth become less of a focus. Faith, vision, and service dwindles, while too many seem more focused on self. However, you can choose. You can choose to ascend in consciousness. So can others and this change can occur just as quickly.

Individually, we are simply the differentiation of the Universal Mind, and who we are and whom we become are brought about by the *Law of Attraction.*

Physical science breaks matter into molecules, molecules into atoms, and atoms into electrons or energy. However, electrons, or energy, appear to be directed by our will or the all-pervading Spirit within us in which we are all united.

All living beings are eternal by the omnipotent power of the Spirit within. The differences in the lives of each of us largely depend upon the level of intelligence we manifest. The greater our understanding and utilization of the Universal Intelligence, the higher scale of being we become or the greater level of success we accomplish.

For example, a dog has a greater level of intelligence and therefore is considered a higher scale of being than a plant. Just as we are a higher scale of being than the dog. The ability to consciously manage our actions and adjust ourselves to our environment is unmatched among all creatures on this earth.

We are created in the image of the Divine and have access to His ultimate power and resources. Our ability to listen to our inner voice, and change direction, when necessary, is crucial to our success in all things, and the Universal Mind responds precisely every time. When we feel something's wrong, that is the Infinite telling us that we are to change course in our direction because our current course or thoughts are off track. We have been given all the intuitive power to communicate with the Divine and adjust our lives and actions according to natural laws.

Natural laws have enabled us to do so many things. The greater our intelligence, the greater our understanding of natural laws, and therefore the greater power we possess because of our ability to recognize and live in alignment with the natural laws. You are simply the individualization of this Universal Intelligence, and the more you understand that the Universal Intelligence permeates everyone and everything, the more you are free, knowing that you have access to this intelligence that is responsive to every demand.

Thought is creative and spiritual. However, all thought does not originate in the individual but in the Universe. You are simply a vessel for Divine thought. The Divine is the source and foundation of your thought, energy, and substance. We are just a vessel for individual expression and creation.

Through thought, we come together with the Divine, where we, as finite beings, unite with the Infinite. Thought is the magic that brings vitality to our physical being and transforms us into one who feels and acts. The Infinite creates through the individual with thought.

Through the *Law of Attraction* that each electron has for every electron, the Divine manifests itself in the physical world. The energy created by thought initiates electrons to come together in form and fulfill the creation of the image in thought.

Everything created is a result of thought attracting and combining electrons into form. This truth has been tested consciously or subconsciously by everyone and continues to prove to be true. This truth's usefulness is directly proportional to your understanding and application of it.

Remember that you are a complete thought entity, meaning you receive only as you give. Growth results from the *Law of Reciprocity*, and like attracts like. The energy produced by thought responds only to the extent of its vibratory harmony.

Therefore, your wealth is seen to be what you inherently are. Affluence in your outer world occurs when you are affluent within. Physical health occurs when you're mentally healthy and happy and being abundantly loved will occur only when you abundantly love others and are filled with love.

"Work like you don't need the money. Love like you've never been hurt. Dance like nobody's watching."

~Mark Twain Samuel Clemens

When you continually give and give, you will continually be given more.

The unlimited power of the Universal Mind will only work to your benefit if you channel the power through constructive thought. This omnipotent power depends upon you understanding it and applying it.

To fully use this unlimited power, you must cultivate the ability to give proper attention through practice. The more attention you give, the greater your interest becomes. The greater your interest, the more attention you give. One follows the other.

To develop a strong interest in anything, pay attention to it consciously. This practice will enable you to cultivate the power of attention and direct your thoughts to manifest your outer world.

The proper understanding of the *Law of Attraction* is nothing more than believing, which has been put to the test and demonstrated to be a fact. It is our living faith or truth.

Meditation Exercise Eighteen

As always, go to your room and take your position. Completely relax and let go of all stress and negativity. Totally relax. Now concentrate upon your power to create. Seek insight and perception and find a logical basis for your faith.

Let the thought dwell on the fact that we, as physical beings, live and move in the external world with air that we must breathe to live. Then let the thought rest on the fact that we as spiritual beings also live and move within a similar but subtler energy upon which we depend for life, and as in the physical world, no life assumes form until after a seed is sown.

In the spiritual world, no effect can be produced until the seed is sown, and the fruit will depend upon the nature of the seed. The result you secure depends upon your perception of the law in the mighty domain of causation, the highest evolution of human consciousness.

The One Creative Principle of Mental Power

Chapter Nineteen

The search for truth is a sympathetic logical process that allows you to understand the cause behind every effect. Every experience is an effect, and the cause is something you can consciously control. Your experiences are not of chance. They are not of your upbringing or the past. Your experience is of destiny that is appropriately directed by your conscious thoughts.

Ultimately, natural laws govern the physical world. If you understand the causes and effects of natural laws, you will be able to use these laws to the benefit of all because you will understand the effect of every cause every time. The laws of gravity, electricity, steam, and cellular service for example, are natural laws that work every single time.

One of those natural laws is that of polarity. Any condition has extremes that are opposite of each other. In the physical world, there are many contrasts. There are hot and cold, North and South, top and bottom, light and dark, front and back, and many other expressions that we use to compare opposites or extremes.

But the two names used are just different labels to describe a single condition and the extremes of that condition. The two labels are relative and are simply two descriptions of a single condition or entity.

Similarly, words are used in the mental and moral worlds to describe two extremes that explain a single condition—good and evil, intelligence and ignorance, and joy and sorrow.

Evil is the absence of good, ignorance is the absence of intelligence, falsity is the absence of truth, and sorrow is the absence of joy. All the negative extremes represent the absence of the respective positive extreme. The positive extremes have vitality and are full of life. When you take away life and love, you don't have anything other than an adverse condition. But life and love give vitality to thought and allow the seeds you plant to grow.

In all of the examples given, the negative can be destroyed by the positive. Light always destroys darkness, truth destroys false, love destroys hate, and intelligence destroys ignorance.

The empowering, loving force of the Universal Mind has vitality and grows and eventually destroys any negative condition.

Realistically, there is only one creative principle, one law, in the physical world as well as the nonphysical world. That is that of the creative energy of the Universal Mind, or the Eternal Energy in which all things are created.

You are related to this creative principle through your ability to think, and your empowering, loving thoughts plant seeds that begin to grow.

The Divine creates through you, the individual, and creation requires a physical world that is forever changing.

When you look at the world today, the buildings, homes, and cars, and compare them to those in the world 100 years ago, not one of them comes close to resembling those of the past, just as it is likely that not one today will resemble those of 100 years from now.

We can look at the same analogy and relate it to the animal kingdom or the plant world. There again, we'll see the same *Law of Change*.

The *Law of Change* still rules the earth when we consider the inorganic world. Mountains appear where there was once a lake. The great cliffs and Yosemite Valley can be traced back to the glaciers that came before the cliffs.

The only thing that will not change is that change is constant and never-ending. This is the Divine continuing to create all things anew. All matter is a result of thought taking form. The incredible power of the Universal Mind, the Infinite working through everything and everyone, ensures that change and creation are never-ending.

However, the Universal Mind is a pure mind in static form or at rest. Our ability to think is our ability to act upon the Universal Mind and convert it from a static mind to a dynamic one. It is thought that is the energy that brings ideas into manifestation through the power of the Universal Mind. It is as if God waits patiently until we act upon His power through thought. Then, with unconditional love, He uses His unlimited resources to deliver what we demand.

Because the Universal Mind is static, it requires energy to start it in motion. Physical energy is furnished by food and correct thinking. The food you eat is converted into energy, enabling you to think. If you stop eating for a long period of time, you will stop thinking. Then you no longer act upon the Universal. There is consequently no action or reaction between you and the Universe. In other words, no cause and effect exist, and the Universal is only pure mind in static form – a mind at rest.

Ultimately, even spiritual activity doesn't occur in the physical world without using physical things such as food for energy.

However, thought constantly and eternally is taking form and is looking for expression. Therefore, in addition to furnishing our bodies with food, we feed our bodies with empowering, loving, constructive thought. Whether you realize it or not, powerful, constructive, empowering, and positive thoughts will be evident in your health, state of mind, business, and environment because your solar plexus expands, supplying energy to every muscle and nerve and beyond. Your vibrational rate aligns with the Universal Substance, attracting all that is required.

When your thoughts are full of weakness, disempowerment, destructiveness, and negativity, they ultimately manifest as some fear, worry, or nervousness and will also be evident in your health, state of mind, business, and environment. Your solar plexus contracts, paralyzing the muscular system. It affects your entire body. Your vibrational rate is not aligned with the Universe, leaving your disempowering thought with you to rot.

There's a belief that physical possessions represent power that will lead to happiness. Although physical possessions represent power, the power fails to compare to mental power.

But what is this mysterious vital force called mental power? Does anyone know?

We don't know, but neither does anyone know what electricity is. We do know that conforming to the requirements of the law by which electricity is governed, it will give us the electrical power we desire. Similarly, we do know that by conforming to the requirements of the law by which mental power is governed, it, too, will give us the power we desire.

Thought that is forced with a finite purpose that serves others is the vital force that allows the seed of thought to grow. Thought is the vital force or energy that has access to unlimited mental power through our unity with the Infinite.

You likely understand at this juncture that everything is energy and even matter is not solid. Matter is composed of particles held together at a high rate of vibration.

The omnipresent substance or Eternal Energy from which all things are created is infinite in quantity and is universally present.

It's easy to look at how light travels and better understand the Eternal Energy that guides it. Light travels about 186,000 miles per second, and some stars that can be seen are so far away that it takes 2000 years for the light to reach earth.

Yet it travels along in waves through the Omnipresent Substance at unbelievable speed. If this can occur, and it clearly can, then it is evident that this Eternal Energy or Omnipresent Substance is universally present.

So how does this Universal Substance manifest in form? All things in this physical world depend upon the rate of vibration and the resulting relationship of atoms to each other. If we want to change the form of manifestation, we have to change the relationship of the atoms to each other, and we do this by changing the rate of vibration.

How do we change the rate of vibration? By changing our thoughts...

Meditation Exercise Nineteen

You are to concentrate. When you concentrate, do so with all that the word implies. Becomes so absorbed in the object of your thought that you are conscious of nothing else and do this a few minutes every day. Become in consciousness what you desire to be.

Take your position and completely still your body and mind, then relax your body and inhibit all undesirable thought. Concentrate on being the person you desire to be. Let the thought rest on the fact that appearances are deceptive. The earth is not flat or stationary, the sky is not a dome, the sun does not move, the stars are not tiny specks of light, and matter, which was once supposed to be fixed, is in a state of perpetual flux.

Realize that the day is fast approaching when modes of thought and action must be adjusted to rapidly increased knowledge of the operation of external principles.

The Omnipresence of God

Chapter Twenty

God is love, and God is omnipresent. True? Most believe so. If this is true, then there is nowhere that God isn't present, wouldn't you agree?

If God is everywhere, then where are Satan and hell? Where is evil?

Most will also agree that we are made in the image and likeness of God, and therefore we must be spiritual beings. Our ability to think is our ability to create; therefore, thinking is a creative process and the activity of the Spirit. God is the Spirit within us, and the Spirit is the creative principle of the Universe. All form is simply the result of the thinking process.

When the creative power of thought is manifested for the benefit of humanity, we call the result good. But when the creative power of thought is manifested destructively, we call the result evil.

This suggests the basis of both good and evil. They are merely words used to describe the quality of the result of the thinking or creative process.

Let's explore the God within each of us. When you say, 'I want to go over there,' who is 'I'? We already know the 'I' is your Spirit. You are a spiritual being, and the Spirit of you is you. Without your Spirit, you'd be nothing.

You could be the wealthiest person on earth. However, if you don't recognize it and if you don't make use of your wealth, it has no value at all. Similarly, it also has no value if you don't recognize or use the Spirit within you.

Thought is your spiritual power. Until you recognize this, you have no power at all. All great things come through our recognition and use of our resources.

You will achieve only temporary superficial results until you recognize the power of thought and consciousness. The more you recognize the spiritual power of thought, the less physical work will be required, and the more inspired thought you will experience.

The secret of the power of thought and consciousness lies in understanding the principles of your mind and your relationship to the Universal Mind. The principles don't change. They're consistent and reliable. The stability offers you an opportunity because you are the vessel for its activity, and therefore you have the power of creation.

The essence of the Universal is within you. It is you. When you recognize this, you will begin to feel the power. You will begin to act as you have never before. It is what will spark the light to your inspiration. It is what gives vitality to your thought. It is what unites you with the invisible forces of the Universe. It is the power that has no fear and leads you down the path to greatness.

You are an imagination workshop, a visualizing entity; what you visualize in your mind's eye in silence will become your great purpose.

Understanding this principle will allow you to use it whenever you require it. Visualize in your mind repeatedly, and the condition in your mind will materialize. True wisdom is being able to call upon the omnipotent power of the Universal Mind on demand.

But if you learn to recognize this inner world that unites with the Universal Forces, and you realize it not only in yourself but in others, in events, in things, and in circumstances, then you will have found the 'Kingdom of Heaven' within.

The power of thought, when understood, can be incredible because it is the secret of all inspiration and genius. It is the most incredible labor-saving device ever dreamed of if used correctly. If misused, it can create disaster and many hours of work.

Every failure we've experienced is a result of the same principle. The principle is unchangeable. It is reliable and consistent. When we picture lack, limitation, poverty, disease, and discord in our minds, we will be delivered the evidence of our thoughts in the outer world.

If you fear an event or an outcome, you can say, 'The thing I feared most has occurred.' If you think mean or ignorant thoughts, you will attract to yourself the result of those thoughts.

When you understand and recognize that the Universal Substance that unites everything and everyone is the source of all power and is within, you tap the source of Divine inspiration.

Inspired thought is the art of self-realization, the art of becoming a vessel for the flow of Infinite wisdom, the art of ideal visualization, and the art of manifestation.

Understand that the Infinite power of the Spirit is omnipresent and, therefore, in the slightest substance and the infinitely large. It permeates all things, even the space and air we breathe. It is present everywhere at all times.

An understanding of this, intellectually and emotionally, will allow you to tap into this power. Your emotional understanding, however, brings vitality to thought.

Therefore, a total understanding is essential to recognize the power of the Spirit within.

I've mentioned many times that inspiration comes in silence and from within. The muscles and nerves must be relaxed. Every part of the physical being must not hinder your ability to receive the inspiration or wisdom necessary to develop your purpose.

Inspired thought comes through your ability to receive these invisible forces, and this art of receiving gives you ultimate power.

You can live more abundantly every time you breathe if you consciously breathe with that intention. The 'if' is a critical condition. The intention directs the attention, and without the attention, you won't secure your desired result. You will get only what you give attention to. You will be supplied with a result equal to your demand.

To receive a more extensive supply, you must increase your demand. Increase your demand for life, energy, love, and vitality, and you will increase your supply.

'In Him, we live and move and have our being.' 'He' is spirit, and He is love. We breathe His life, love, and spirit every time we breathe. His spirit is the Eternal Energy with which we could not exist for a moment without. It is the life of the solar plexus.

Every time we breathe, we fill our lungs with His spirit and visualize our body with this Eternal Energy, which is life itself. This is how we can make a conscious connection with all life, all wisdom, and all substance.

This breath of life is the Universal Substance, and our conscious unity with it allows us to focus and exercise the power of His creative energy. This creative power comes through thought, and the quality of your thoughts will determine the quality of the resulting condition.

Every time you think, you start a progression of causes that will create a condition and faithful harmony with the quality of the thought. Thought, which is in harmony with the Universal Mind, will result in quality conditions. Thought that is destructive to yourself or others will result in conditions that are destructive to you.

You can use thought constructively or destructively. However, the law will not allow a destructive thought to produce a constructive result or a constructive thought to produce a destructive result. Think constructively and get constructive results. Think destructively and get destructive results.

You are free. Yes, you are free right now. You have a choice to use this incredible creative power as you will. You're in the driver's seat. You make the decision. It is your will. However, you must also be prepared, either way, for the consequences.

This is the danger of free will. Some believe that they can plant a seed of thought of one kind and, by their will, make it grow into the result of another. The idea that you can compel compliance by using your power is destined for failure as it alienates the power of the Universal Mind, which is the same power you are seeking to use.

Imagine the individual attempting to force the Divine. The finite in conflict with the Infinite. This is guaranteed to fail and is as inevitable as our well-being is guaranteed when we work in cooperation with the Divine and all that is good.

Meditation Exercise Twenty

Go into the silence and concentrate on the fact that 'In Him, we live and move and have our being' is literally and scientifically exact. That you are because He is, that if He is omnipresent, He must be in you. If He is, all in all, you must be in Him. He is spirit, and you are made in His image and likeness; the only difference between His spirit and your spirit is one of degree.

When you realize this clearly, you will have found the secret of the creative power of thought. You will have found the origin of both good and evil. You will have found the secret of the incredible power of concentration. It's the solution to every problem, whether physical, financial, or environmental.

The power to think constructively, deeply, and clearly is an acknowledged and deadly enemy to mistakes and blunders, superstitions, unscientific theories, and irrational beliefs.

The Big Thoughts

Chapter Twenty-One

The Universal Mind is unconditional; it's limitless. The more we recognize our unity with the Universal Mind, the more we understand that there are no limitations. The more we recognize no limitations, the more we become free.

As soon as you recognize this unlimited power within you, you begin to create the cultivation of this power, and whatever you recognize to be true always manifests in your physical world.

The Infinite Mind is the source of all things. There's only one, and it is indestructible. You are a passage in which this

Universal Substance is being manifested. Your ability to think is your ability to use the power of the Universal Substance and create in your physical world.

"Your only limitations are those you set up in your mind or permit others to set up for you."

~Og Mandino

This is awesome! This means we have no limitations on the quality, quantity, and possibilities available to us. Use the analogy of an electrical wire that is hot or live, which will represent the Universal Mind. Now take any dead electrical wire without current, which represents each individual. All that must happen for the dead wire to have all the power of the live wire is for the dead wire to come in contact with the live wire. Instantly, the dead wire that had nothing now has all the power it needs.

The way you acquire all the power you need to master every situation is to become aware of your unity with the All-Powerful. The more you become aware of your unity with the All-Powerful, the easier it becomes to control your thoughts in a manner that will eliminate every undesirable condition in your physical world.

Big ideas seem to overshadow small ideas, to the point of smothering them and making them irrelevant. This makes it easy for you to instantaneously destroy all small, undesirable, trivial, irritating obstacles. Keep your ideas big. Not only do you eliminate the small stuff that clutters your results, but it brings you in alignment with global thought, which will increase your mental capacity and improve your ability to accomplish things of significance.

The creative power of the Universal Mind has no difficulty handling big projects, as it is just as present and huge as in the small ones. This is one of the secrets to success. Think big thoughts. When you realize the creative power of the Universal Mind, you understand how you can bring about any condition by creating the desirable condition in your mind. Any condition held in consciousness for any time eventually impresses upon the subconscious mind an imprint that the Eternal Energy will surge into your physical world.

This is how you produce desired results. The results are simply the reflection of your predominant thoughts, a mere image of who you are in consciousness, your attitude.

"Life reflects your thoughts back to you."

You have learned that your predominant thoughts make imprints on the subconscious mind. These imprints create predispositions that create character, skill, and purpose. The combination of character, skill, and purpose determines the experiences you will have in life.

The experiences that result are due to the *Law of Attraction.* The experience you hold in your mind's eye, or your inner world, attracts a corresponding experience in your outer world.

Your predominant thought is your mental magnet, and the law is that 'like creates like.' Your mental attitude will attract a corresponding condition in this physical world.

Your mental attitude is your personality and is composed of the thoughts that you have been creating in your mind. Therefore, if you want conditions to change, you change your thoughts. This results in a change in your mental attitude, which changes your personality and everything you experience in life.

This sounds easy, but it can be pretty tricky. Your mental attitude is a mere image of the mental pictures you've been giving your brain. If you don't like what you've been giving your brain, create new pictures through the art of visualization and persist until you become in consciousness what you desire to be.

As soon as you change the pictures in your mind, you will begin to change the pictures representing your environment in your physical world. Hold the perfect picture of your desire in your mind until your picture objectifies in the outer world.

If your desired result requires an attitude or resource that you don't currently have today, that's OK. Build it into your picture. Picture all the essentials. They are a critical part of your picture. Include the appropriate feelings. Feelings combined with thought create the irresistible magnetic power that attracts the things you desire. Your feelings give your pictures life, and your life allows things to grow.

Please don't set your sights low; set them high. Make them big; give them purpose. Seek the highest levels because there is nothing too big for the forces of the Universal Mind.

Now make it a habit. Make new habits that result in correct thinking and break old habits of incorrect thinking. All habits are formed by doing. You do something, then you do it again, and you do it repeatedly, and soon you have a habit. Well, that's also exactly how you break habits. If you stop doing something repeatedly, you will break habits as well. Failing now and then is no reason to quit entirely, as one indiscretion now and then will not be powerful enough to overtake your multiple impressions.

There are only two classes of people. Who are you?

Do you look forward or look back? There is no standing still in this world as it is always progressing. If you aren't progressing, then you're going backward. You are either progressing or digressing, continuing to improve or getting worse; you are moving forward or backward. Which is it for you?

"We can draw lessons from the past.
but we cannot live in it."

~Lyndon B Johnson

Are you going to be creating, or one who prefers precedent to progress? You must decide which one you will be. Are you going to look forward and create in your inner world, or look backward and live your future based on past patterns?

Live to create, be part of a better world, and be happy.

We are in a transition. The old way of thinking must make way for progress. When we realize that God is within and that it is through him that all things are possible, and it is with love that the *Law of Growth* responds, then we can frame laws that consider the liberties and rights of all versus the privileged few.

The real interest of democracy is to recognize the divinity of the human spirit. Recognize that all power comes from within and is a result of our unity with the Divine. Not one of us has any more power than any other, except by our surrender of such power; there is no such thing as the doctrine of Divine election. The Divine has no favorites and makes no exceptions. The Divine delivers in the outer world what correlates to your inner world every time for everyone.

When you understand and realize your unity with the Divine and the power of the Universal Mind, the Universal Principle will work in your favor because you will have found the source of all health, wealth, love, and power.

"All things are possible to him who believes."

~ Mark 9: 23

The only limits you have are those you impose upon yourself, as there are no limits to the creative power of the Universal Mind. Dare to believe. Dare to dream. Think of your ideal as an already accomplished fact. Become it in consciousness. Believe!

Meditation Exercise Twenty-One

Take your position and relax your body and mind, and inhibit all undesirable thought. Then concentrate on the truth. Try to realize that the truth shall make you free. The truth is that nothing can permanently stand in your way of success when you learn to apply scientifically correct thought methods and principles. Realize that you are manifesting in your physical world your natural soul forces. Realize that silence offers an ever-available and almost unlimited opportunity for awakening the highest conception of truth.

Focus in silence. Comprehend the omnipotence itself in absolute silence. Silent thought concentration is the proper method of reaching, awakening, and then expressing the extraordinary potential power of the world within.

Our Healing Powers

Chapter Twenty-Two

Two distinct methods carry on the life processes. First is our intake, our ability to use the food and drink we consume. Nutrients are necessary to construct cells. Second is our ability to discard all the leftovers. Our bodies break down and dispose of waste material.

Food, water, and air are the only things necessary to construct cells. This being the case, you might think it would be simple to prolong life. However, it's more complicated. Waste material must effectively and efficiently be discarded. Waste accumulates and saturates the tissues causing autointoxication, which results in illness. In some cases, this order is local, and in others, it can affect your entire body.

Therefore, the secret to good health is as easy as providing our bodies with the proper nutrients and effectively disposing of all waste. The first is much simpler than the second.

To properly dispose of waste material, we must be able to increase the flow and distribution of vital energy throughout our body, and this can only be done by eliminating thoughts of fear, worry, anxiety, jealousy, hatred, and every other destructive thought, which tend to tear down and destroy the nerves and glands that control the excretion and elimination of poisonous and waste matter.

Consider that what we are today is entirely the result of our past thinking. Our character, environment, ability, and physical condition result from our past thoughts. Applying knowledge is how we can make our future whatever we desire it to be.

If you're overweight or your health is not what you want it to be, let's examine your way of thinking. Remember that every thought leaves an impression in your subconscious mind. Every impression plants a seed of thought that begins to grow, and before you know it, you have a health issue if you have disempowering thoughts. Negativity and destructive thoughts contract the solar plexus, which depletes the amount of energy to all your muscles and nerves.

If your current thoughts are negative, what would grow will be sickness, decay, and failure. The question is, what are you thinking? What are you creating? What is the crop that you're harvesting?

Empowering, constructive thoughts expand the solar plexus, which provides additional energy to the muscles and nerves throughout the body. What is considered by many the most effective way to plant the spiritually empowering seed of thought that grows into a fully energized body is visualization.

I can't say this enough. Visualize in your mind's eye the image of perfect health. Keep it a vivid thought. Hold it in your mind's eye until your consciousness completely accepts it. There have been many miracles, as some would call them, through mental imagery. Thousands have overcome physical illnesses and diseases by this method in a few days and sometimes in just a few minutes.

Every time you have a thought, there is a vibration. All form is a mode of vibration. Therefore, anytime you have a thought, you create a vibration that modifies every atom in the body. Every living cell is affected, and there is a chemical change in every group of living cells. Through the *Law of Vibration*, the mind exercises control over the body.

Everything in the Universe is what it is because of its rate of vibration. If we change the rate of vibration, we change the nature, quality, and form. Everything in the Universe is constantly changing because the rate of vibration is constantly changing. Since thought is also a vibration, we can influence changes in existing vibrations with the vibration of our thoughts.

You already have this power and are using it successfully with every thought. The problem, however, is that we often need to direct this power consciously. It is time to use this power to produce only desirable results intelligently. This is easier than it sounds. You know what feels good, and you know what feels bad, right?

Think about times when you felt excited, courageous, kind or any other feeling that felt good. These empowering thoughts created vibrations that brought about desirable results. Remember when you were filled with envy, hatred, jealousy, or depression. Your feelings didn't feel good. Now remember the result, not the short-term results, but the end result.

In situations where you had empowering thoughts that felt good, the result was likely mental, moral, and physical health. In situations where you had disempowering thoughts that you knew didn't feel right, the result was likely dissension, disagreement, and illness. Understand that this is a universal law. We have this power to control our destiny and co-create with the Divine.

The conscious mind directly results in effects on the body. Think about a time when you told an excellent joke and began to laugh hysterically. Your thought controlled that response and ultimately controlled the muscles of your body. If you didn't think it was funny, you didn't laugh. If you thought it was funny, you laughed. In either case, your conscious thought controlled this physical response.

If a situation occurs that prompts sympathy; your eyes begin to water. Sometimes you can't even control this response. You feel something, and your body instantly responds. Thought controls the glands in your body too.

If someone says something to you that angers you, your face begins to turn red, and your blood pressure rises. Your thoughts have some control over the circulation of your blood.

All these examples are your conscious thought immediately affecting your body's muscles, glands, and blood circulation. Conscious thought caused these effects. Because it's conscious thought, as soon as you change your thought, these effects will dissipate.

But what happens when the subconscious mind controls the body? You cut your finger, and immediately thousands of cells begin working to heal this wound, and within days, your cut is nothing but a minor scar, if that.

You break a bone, and again, your body begins repairing, and within a few weeks, your bone is healed. No procedure on earth can cure the way your subconscious mind can.

What happens if you swallow poison? Your subconscious immediately recognizes a problem, and your body will attempt to get rid of it immediately. Your subconscious mind is always working, and you are a self-healing machine.

All these self-healing examples happen without conscious thought. Our bodies self-heal perfectly if we don't interfere with the healing process. The millions of cells in your body are all intelligent and instinctively immediately begin repairing or correcting any illness or disease.

However, these cells respond to your conscious thoughts as well.[11] Unfortunately, our cells are often paralyzed and become impotent by our thoughts of fear, doubt, and anxiety. They are like an army ready, willing, and able, just waiting for the command to cure. But thoughts of illness paralyze them instead at times.

Our way to perfect health is based on the *Law of Vibration*, controlled by the mind. Treating symptoms, or the external ones, without changing your thoughts will result only in a lack of results. The inner world must change for an illness to be cured.

The cause is always within; therefore, to change the effect, we must change the inner cause by changing our thoughts.

The millions of cells in your body are intelligent and will respond to your direction of thought. Your cells are all creators and will create the configuration you direct through your thoughts. Therefore, when you picture perfect images of health in your mind, the creative energy of your intelligent cells will build a body of perfect health.

Your mental attitude controls the quality of the brain cells. If you have a negative mental attitude, your subconscious mind will transfer this to your body. If you have a positive mental attitude, this also will be transferred to your body. To manifest health and vitality, you must think empowering thoughts, which result in the radiation of energy throughout your body.

Every part of the human body and everything in the Universe results from the rate of vibration. Mental action is a rate of vibration. And a higher rate of vibration controls or destroys a lower rate of vibration.

You can make any physical condition in your body change. You picture the perfect physical body and condition and impress upon your subconscious this vision so deeply that you plant the seed of spiritual thought. This begins to grow and creates high- quality brain cells, and the brain cells' character determines the vibration rate. The higher the quality of the brain cells, the higher the vibration, and a higher vibration destroys a lower vibration. The result is an improved physical condition.

There is practically no limitation on our ability to place ourselves in harmony with natural law, which is omnipotent.

Although it is still seldom spoken of by physicians, it is becoming more and more evident that the mind has power and control over the body. There is no doubt that few are aware of how much they can do for themselves when they are ill or with a disease. We have the power to heal any ailment. Mental therapeutics is something all of us can do. We can bring about healing by calming the mind or prompting feelings of pleasure, hope, faith, and love. By occupying the mind with mental work and diverting our thoughts from illness and disease to anything that brings pleasure and love, we have the omnipotent healing power of the Divine within.

Meditation Exercise Twenty-Two

Relax your mind and body and concentrate on this quote by Alfred Lord Tennyson, "Speak to Him, thou for He hears, and Spirit with Spirit can meet. Closer is he than breathing, and nearer than hands and feet." Then try to realize that when you do speak to Him, you are in touch with omnipotence, the All-Powerful.

Realize that this power is also omnipresent and will quickly destroy any and every form of sickness or suffering and substitute harmony and perfection. Thoughts that align and recognize this unlimited power attract all you need.

Some seem to think that God sends illness and suffering. Recognize that this cannot be so because then every physician, every surgeon, and every nurse is defying the will of God. Of course, this quickly reasons itself into absurdity. Let the thought rest on the fact that until recently, theology has been trying to teach an impossible Creator, a Creator who created beings capable of sinning and then allowing them to be eternally punished for such sins. The outcome of these teachings created fear instead of love, and so, after 2000 years, theology has now redirected these teachings.

Appreciate yourself and all. You are made in the image and likeness of God, and you will more readily appreciate the all- originating mind that forms, upholds, sustains, originates, and creates all there is. All are parts of one stupendous whole, whose body nature is, and God the soul.

Financial Abundance

Chapter Twenty-Three

Success is a journey, not a destination. The joy and fun we receive are in the pursuit of our goals, and the achievement of what we desire rather than the possession itself. It's a continuous journey toward the achievement of predetermined, worthwhile goals. As we achieve our goals, we must determine what we would like to pursue next, and we can quickly determine what's next by keeping an open mind and reaching out for the new.

The first principle of success is service to others. We get what we give. Therefore, it should be a pleasure to be able to give to others. The first principle of financial success is financial service to others. There is no difference when you apply success principles to your finances.

> *"One of the things I keep learning is that the secret*
> *of being happy is doing things for other people."*
>
> ~Dick Gregory

To become a money magnet, you must include in your plans how you can assist in the financial well-being of others. The more you help others achieve financial abundance, the more money you will attract. When your thoughts and plans include financial benefits for everyone, you achieve financial success for yourself.

The *Law of Cause and Effect* guarantees that you must receive something in exchange whenever you project anything into the Universe. Therefore, unselfish, optimistic, and constructive thoughts will have a much more significant positive effect than pessimistic, destructive, selfish thoughts.

Money is an essential resource in our physical world, and generous thought, considering the benefits of all involved, is filled with vitality. The *Law of Growth* will ensure that this generosity expands, permeating your physical world.

Selfish thought, considering benefits only to you, will contract, collapse, and ultimately die.

When you recognize the omnipotent power abundant in all things, adjust your thought to know that there is plenty for all, and be of service to others, then you will always attract all that you desire.

The wealthiest people in the world did not get that way because of their ability to influence others to lose money or resources. It is quite the opposite. It is because they helped others earn money. The more you are of service to others, and assist others in acquiring wealth and abundance, the more financial abundance you will attract into your own life.

You must hold the things you desire in consciousness to attract all you desire. When it comes to money, there is no exception. Money consciousness is a state of mind. You must be open to all the abundance the Universe offers and act with faith, courage, and enthusiasm when given the opportunity. This does not mean you act blindly, but when a door is open, and it's clear that it leads to what you desire, you are then to walk briskly, yet vigilantly, through the door.

Poverty consciousness is usually caused by fear. If we concentrate on what we fear, we get what we fear.

It is no accident that a small percentage of the population carries most of the wealth and power. Unfortunately, most people accept past precedents and the ideas of others instead of tapping into their power of creative thought within.

Your will directs concentration. You have the conscious power to decide what to think about. If you concentrate on sorrow, discord, and loss, since thought is creative, this concentration leads to more sorrow, discord, and loss. On the other hand, if you concentrate on joy, success, and gain, the creative power of thought will lead to more joy, success, and gain. This principle can be used in business just as easily as any other desire.

All things that are lasting successes are the result of thought, and you have a direct connection with the Infinite

Mind. The Infinite Mind has unlimited possibilities and fantastic ideas that you can put into practical use.

If you take away human nature, what is left is the understanding of an Infinite Presence and Power, the perfect example of which is consciousness – Spirit. It is no surprise that since we are Spirit, we can harmonize with the Infinite to manifest a minor degree of the All-Powerful.

You draw upon the Infinite supply of your ideas, as the Spirit is the soul of consciousness and the source of all ideas. When you realize the true understanding of your Spirit, you will recognize that its laws of manifestation are the most practical thing you can find and are the fundamental nature of all achievement.

If you can find your direct connection with the Infinite Mind or the Spirit and think of big ideas for serving others, you will find financial success.

In application, you use the creative power of thought to build an idealistic vision of what you desire to manifest. By giving your attention to thought, you develop concentration. You can fill in the details of your idealistic vision or change or improve your idea from time to time, proceeding from the initial idea to the finished detail. This power can be applied to anything, including financial wealth and business.

By giving attention to your thoughts in this manner, you develop concentration, and concentration develops spiritual power. Spiritual power is the most substantial influence in existence.

Some may question whether using spiritual power to manifest financial success is an acceptable behavior. Understand that if the Infinite objected, then it wouldn't work. Only that which is in harmony with the Infinite expands and materializes.

Therefore, the power of Spirit is reasonably practical and is the creative activity behind every beneficial activity. It is the Spirit that easily controls and forms matter. Nothing provides more practical value than our thought, which is united with the power of Spirit. Our spirituality is the only absolutely practical thing there is.

Meditation Exercise Twenty-Three

Relax and clear your mind, then concentrate on the fact that you are not a body with a spirit but a spirit with a body. For this reason, your desires are incapable of any permanent satisfaction in anything that is not spiritual.

Money is, therefore, of no value except to bring about the conditions you desire, which must be harmonious. Harmonious conditions necessitate sufficient supply so that if there appears to be any lack, we should realize that the idea or soul of money is service. As this thought takes form, channels of supply will be opened, and you will have the satisfaction of knowing that spiritual methods are entirely practical.

Leave a 1-Click Review!

Customer reviews

☆☆☆☆☆ 5 out of 5

141 global ratings

5 star		97%
4 star		3%
3 star		0%
2 star		0%
1 star		0%

˅ How customer reviews and ratings work

Review this product

Share your thoughts with other customers

Write a customer review

I would be incredibly thankful if you could take just 60 seconds to write a brief review on Amazon, even if it's just a few sentences.

>> Click here to leave a quick review

The Truth Shall Make You Free

Chapter Twenty-Four

Vibrations are everywhere and amazing. When we hear a noise, it is a vibration that causes a sound to be heard in our minds. We hear sounds that produce vibrations up to 38,000 per second. When the vibration rate exceeds 38,000 per second, we can no longer hear a sound. However, this doesn't mean that there is no sound. It just means that our minds cannot create the sound associated with the vibration.

When we see light, this is also a vibration that, when translated by our eyes, causes light to be seen in our minds. We see light when the vibration rate is at 400 trillion a second. As the vibration rate increases, our eyes translate the vibration into colors.

As the vibration rate drops, our sense of touch translates the vibration as heat.

All these sensations are forms of energy that produce vibrations, and our senses interpret the vibrations as sounds, sites, and feelings. Yet the interpretations occur as sounds, sites, and feelings only in our minds, not in our physical world.

It is clear then that our senses don't tell us the truth about our physical world. If they did, we would believe that the sun moves, and that the world is flat. We must look beyond our five senses to understand the truth.

To have abundance in all things in life, you must know the truth and reverse the evidence of the senses. Reverse the evidence of the senses means that you must think about harmony when there is discord. When there is illness, you must think about health. When there is a lack, you must think of abundance.

Every form of discord, illness, and lack is simply the result of wrong thinking, and correct thinking will correct any undesirable condition that isn't consistent with truth. When you recognize this truth, the truth shall make you free.

Your goal must be to convince yourself of this truth. When you have succeeded in doing so, the truth and your correct thinking will manifest themselves.

The power of your spirit makes this so. Spirit is perfect, strong, powerful, harmonious, and joyous. This truth and thought create the highest rate of vibration there is, and therefore it annihilates every form of incorrect thinking in the same way that light destroys darkness.

The only activity the Spirit within possesses is the power to think; since the Spirit is creative, thought must be creative. When you think the truth, you create what is true; when truth manifests, what is false must cease to exist. Your ability to think is ultimately your ability to use the omnipotent power for the benefit of yourself and others.

When using the word 'God,' most people consider this word to mean something outside of themselves. Yet precisely the opposite is true. It is God or the Spirit within us that is our very life. Without it, we would be dead. As soon as the Spirit leaves the body, the body dies. Therefore, the Spirit is all there is to our living beings.

This truth will enable you to overcome every form of lack, limitation, or illness. The outer world is relative only. The truth is absolute and found only from within us.

It is essential to train your mind to see truth only. Express in your mind true conditions only. The truth is that the spirit or the 'I' within you is perfect, whole, powerful, joyous, and harmonious. It can never have any lack or limitation. Genius and greatness are within us, which come from the Spirit within us—the Spirit, which is one with the Universal Mind.

This truth makes you free, and the conscious knowledge of this truth will allow you to overcome any undesirable condition.

All conditions you experience are created by thought. Therefore, discord, illness, and lack are mental conditions in which you fail to perceive the truth. You must look within and discover the mental error to determine the cause behind any undesirable condition. Your condition will be corrected as soon as you correct your thinking and focus on the truth.

Your physical world will be a mere reflection of your inner world. If you see limitation, lack, imperfection, illness, and destruction, you will experience it. Conversely, if you see abundance, Infinite possibilities, perfection, health, and harmony, you will also experience it.

Everything you are experiencing in your life right now already lives in your subconscious personality, which attracts to it the mental and physical conditions that are agreeable to its personality. Therefore, who you are in your subconscious determines your future, and who you were in your subconscious determined your present.

It doesn't matter what the difficulty is, where it is, or who is affected; you must convince yourself of the truth you desire to see manifest.

The conditions in your outer world result from the conditions in your inner world. Meditation, or prayer if you prefer, when done correctly, will remove any undesirable condition. You must form a mental picture of the condition desired. By holding the perfect ideal in your mind, you can bring about the perfect ideal in your physical world.

Additionally, you can create self-talk or argue against the irrational thoughts that created the undesirable condition, to begin with. Every form of concentration, mental imaging, self-talk, and subliminal auto suggestion is simply a way by which you persuade yourself to realize the truth. However, imagining the desirable condition is the most effective and efficient way to correct any undesirable condition.

Every time you allow your thoughts to rest on any inharmonious condition realize that the condition is only perception and has no reality. Focus on truth.

The Universal Mind in which 'we live and move and have our being' is one and indivisible, and therefore it is possible to help others as to help ourselves. All minds are one mind; this is one of the most challenging concepts to grasp.

To create abundance where there is lack or destroy limitations where there are others involved, you don't need to focus on the others but on driving any belief of lack or limitation out of your mind. The key is clear, decisive, calm, deliberate, and sustained thought with a definite end desirable vision. The result will be accomplished as soon as you have succeeded in doing this.

When you realize this truth, you will have come into possession of the *Master Key*.

You can get out of life precisely what you desire by first putting into life what you desire. The result of this knowledge is the truth that makes us free, not only free from every lack and limitation but free from sorrow and worry. This is the truth that applies to everyone.

If your beliefs are geared toward religion, Jesus, the greatest religious teacher of the world, as well as many other great religious teachers, has shown us the way so clearly for us to follow.

If your beliefs are geared toward physical science, the law will operate with mathematical certainty.

In any regard, understanding this principle is the secret that explains how gold in the mind creates gold in the heart and in the hand. It is the secret that enables you to reach degrees of power that may, to some, seem impossible.

You will also be able to say; it is not I that does the work, but the Father that dwells within me. He does the work. You will understand that the Father is the Universal Mind and that He really and truly dwells within you. You will recognize that the beautiful promise made in the Bible is fact, not fiction, and can be demonstrated by anyone having sufficient understanding. You will know that faith believes this truth.

Meditation Exercise Twenty-Four

For your last exercise, begin as always by taking your position and relaxing your body and mind. Now realize that this is truly a wonderful world in which we live, you are a wonderful being, and many are awakening to a knowledge of the truth. As fast as they awake, they will realize the splendors that exist for those who find themselves in the promised land.

They have crossed the river of judgment and have arrived at the point of discrimination between the true and the false and have found that all they have ever willed or dreamed was but a fragment of the true nature of this dazzling reality.

About the Author

Charles Haanel (b. May 22, 1866; d. November 27, 1949) and Tammy Gallagher (b. March 16, 1964), are technically co-authors. The inspiration of each chapter and their corresponding mediation exercises come from the original *Master Key*. Charles and Tammy's time spent on this earth did not overlap, and they therefore have never had an opportunity to meet. About the only thing the two authors have in common is that they were born in Michigan, were Republicans, and developed the fun interest in the power within.[13]

Haanel, born in Ann Arbor MI, was the son of Hugo and Ameline Haanel.[13] The family moved to Saint Louis when Charles was a child. Charles entered the business world as an office boy for the national enameling and stapling company, for which he worked for 15 years. Haanel resigned his position and organized a company in 1889 that raised sugar and coffee, of which he was made president. The plantation was successful from the beginning and grew to be a company of significant financial worth.

Charles organized the continental commercial company, and ran this business as its president. He was one of the organizers of the Sacramento Valley Improvement company and from the beginning was its president as well.

In 1885, Charles married miss Esther M Smith. 6 years later, Esther's death left Charles a widower with one son and two daughters. Charles remarried, to miss Margaret Nicholson, in 1908.[13]

Although Charles was a republican, his business interests left no time for him to take an active interest in politics beyond voting and using his influence to assist those candidates he supported.

Charles was a member of Keystone Lodge, a 32nd degree Mason, and a Shriner. He was also affiliated with the Missouri Athletic Club.

Haanel could take a calm survey of life and correcting valuing it's opportunities, possibilities, demands, and obligations. He had wisely sought success along the lines of least resistance, and yet when difficulties and obstacles confronted him, he displayed a force of character that enabled him to overcome them and continue on the pathway to prosperity.

Tammy Gallagher, born in Detroit MI, is the daughter of Dominic Cinquemani and Barbara woods. Tammy remained in Michigan with her family through her youth and spent most of her childhood in St Clair Shores, MI. Tammy's father died when she was five years old, and her mother remarried, Warren woods, when Tammy was fifteen.

Tammy began working as a cashier that year at a local fruit market and worked two jobs during college until she decided to quit college and move to Tampa, Florida to become a reservation sales agent with the small commuter airline. Within a year, the company filed for bankruptcy, and

Tammy became a travel agent for a short period of time before she joined Telecredit as a consumer relations representative. Tammy remained with Telecredit, was promoted many times, and ultimately became an outside sales representative. It was here where she remained until the events described in the Introduction.

Life has a way of leading us to our fate, and Tammy Gallagher's life was no exception. She became overweight in her twenties, developed high blood pressure and high cholesterol, and developed Crohn's disease in her late forties. She spent most of her adult life in the residential development industry but found herself leaving the industry in 2018 as she realized she was trading her health for money. She was operating on autopilot and wasn't happy, so she sought to change.

Tammy has learned that 'giving up' is never an option, and she finally returned to college in her fifties to get the degree she wanted. Tammy is a functional nutrition and lifestyle practitioner and author; best yet, she received her health and life back. She now shares the wisdom gained from her experience and education with others as a means of encouragement and support.

In 2018 Tammy decided that she wanted to give back more to the world than she had been able to do by continuing her journey toward mastering a healthy body and mind. She opened Ballantyne Weight Loss Center to help others achieve health as well.

As a businesswoman, Tammy understands that changing one's life requires vision, determination, and perseverance. This book aims to provide people with inspiration and advice on how to reinvent yourself to live a happier, healthier, more fulfilled life.

Resources

1. Charles F. Haanel. (2020, June 26). *The History of The Master Key System and Its Influence | Charles F. Haanel.* Charles F. Haanel | the Man Who Unlocked the World, the Author of the Master Key System, and the Father of Personal Development. Retrieved October 12, 2022, from https://www.haanel.com/history-influence/

2. Hopkins, T. (1982, September 29). *The Official Guide to Success, V. 1: Tom Hopkins' Personal Success Program.* Hopkins.

3. Wikipedia contributors. (2022, September 27). *Enteric nervous system.* Wikipedia. Retrieved October 12, 2022,

   from
   https://en.wikipedia.org/wiki/Enteric_nervous_system

4. Woo, C. (2021, October 15). *Our second brain: More than a gut feeling.* UBC Neuroscience. Retrieved October 12, 2022, from https://neuroscience.ubc.ca/our-second-brain-more-than-a-gut-feeling/

5. Hopkins, T. (1982, September 29). *The Official Guide to Success, V. 1: Tom Hopkins' Personal Success Program.* Hopkins.

6. Abraham, Hicks, J., & Hicks, J. (2004). *Ask and it is Given: Learning to Manifest Your Desires.* Penguin Random House.

7. Vasković, J., MD. (2022, July 6). *Celiac plexus.* Kenhub. Retrieved October 15, 2022, from https://www.kenhub.com/en/library/anatomy/celiac-plexus

8. Kristin. (2022, August 24). *How to Heal & Open Your Solar Plexus Chakra.* Be My Travel Muse. Retrieved October 15, 2022, from https://www.bemytravelmuse.com/solar-plexus-chakra/

9. Bryant, C. (n.d.). *The relationship between attitudes to aging and physical and mental health in older adults |*

International Psychogeriatrics. Cambridge Core. Retrieved October 15, 2022, from https://www.cambridge.org/core/journals/international-psychogeriatrics/article/abs/relationship-between-attitudes-to-aging-and-physical-and-mental-health-in-older-adults/5824A4FC3E98C7DD65F6A4BC0E68E98F

10. *Stress, Anxiety and Your Immune System: How to Avoid Getting Sick | Hartford HealthCare | CT.* (n.d.). Retrieved October 16, 2022, from https://hartfordhealthcare.org/about-us/news-press/news-detail?articleId=18853

11. Cook, G. (2016, January 19). *The Science of Healing Thoughts.* Scientific American. https://www.scientificamerican.com/article/the-science-of-healing-thoughts/

12. O'Connell, C. (2021, April 16). *Quantum physics for the terminally confused.* Cosmos. https://cosmosmagazine.com/science/physics/quantum-physics-for-the-terminally-confused/

13. Charles F. Haanel. (2021, November 24). In *Wikipedia.* https://en.wikipedia.org/wiki/Charles_F._Haanel

Get Free eBooks

If you'd like EARLY and FREE e-books written by Tammy Gallagher or published by TamGall Publishing, sign up here:

tamgall.com/book-reviewers

Leave a Review!

Customer reviews

⭐⭐⭐⭐⭐ 5 out of 5

141 global ratings

5 star	████████████	97%
4 star	▏	3%
3 star		0%
2 star		0%
1 star		0%

⌄ How customer reviews and ratings work

Review this product

Share your thoughts with other customers

Write a customer review

I would be incredibly thankful if you would take just 60 seconds to write a brief review on Amazon, even if it's just a few sentences.

tinyurl.com/guide-sm

Just for You!

A FREE GIFT FOR OUR READERS

Get my free eBook on sweeteners...the good, the bad and the ugly. Which sweeteners to avoid and which provide health benefits.

Visit *www.tamgall.com/sweeteners-ebook*

www.ingramcontent.com/pod-product-compliance
Lightning Source LLC
Chambersburg PA
CBHW061130120626
46546CB00005B/1729